BRITAIN'S
GREAT WAR
EXPERIENCE

Other titles from Peter Liddle
and in print with Pen & Sword:

At the Eleventh Hour

Passchendaele in Perspective

Facing Armageddon

The Soldier's War

D-Day - By Those Who Were There

Captured Memories 1900–1918

Captured Memories 1930–1945

The Gallipoli Experience Reconsidered*

* To be published February 2015

BRITAIN'S GREAT WAR EXPERIENCE

LIFE AT HOME AND ABROAD
1914-1918

PETER LIDDLE

Pen & Sword
MILITARY

First published in Great Britain in 1994
under the title The Worst Ordeal by Leo Cooper

Reprinted in this format in 2014 by
Pen & Sword Military
An imprint of
Pen & Sword Books Ltd
47 Church Street
Barnsley, South Yorkshire
S70 2AS

ISBN 978 1 47382 116 3

A CIP catalogue record for this book is available from the British Library

Printed and bound in England
By CPI Group (UK) Ltd, Croydon, CR0 4YY

Pen & Sword Books Ltd incorporates the Imprints of Aviation, Atlas,
Family History, Fiction, Maritime, Military, Discovery, Politics, History,
Archaeology, Select, Wharncliffe Local History, Wharncliffe True Crime,
Military Classics, Wharncliffe Transport, Leo Cooper, The Praetorian Press,
Remember When, Seaforth Publishing and Frontline Publishing

For a complete list of Pen & Sword titles please contact
PEN & SWORD BOOKS LIMITED
47 Church Street, Barnsley, South Yorkshire, S70 2AS, England
E-mail: enquiries@pen-and-sword.co.uk
Website: www.pen-and-sword.co.uk

CONTENTS

Acknowledgements

As Keeper of the Liddle Collection, the collection of war-related materials in the Library in the University of Leeds, I am fortunate in receiving all manner of voluntary assistance. First and Second World War men are tape-recorded, memorabilia is collected and delivered to the University and original documents are processed, catalogued and cross-referred by more than thirty people who operate with team spirit even though some have never met. Behind this team there is an association of Friends of the Collection, the members of which are valued for the supportive work they undertake and particularly in their promotion of the Collection as a fitting repository for the preservation of personal papers or souvenirs related to periods of 19th and 20th century conflict.

Some of these Friends, in addition to their work for the Collection, have helped me in the preparation of this book. Isabel Farrell in Lenzie, Strathkelvin, Adam Smith of Burnley and currently a post-graduate student at St Andrews University, Gwennyth Gibson and Ron Gormley of Sunderland, Albert Smith of Wakefield, Tim Whitcombe of Bradford, Elnora Ferguson in Birmingham, John Richards near Cardiff, Ian Whitehead of Chorlton-cum-Hardy and now in the History Department of the University of Derby, Ann Clayton in Liverpool, Bill Turner in Accrington, busy people in every case, have generously given me their time either researching in regionally based archives or working here in Leeds.

Working class images were a principal area of concern in preparing this book and here the help of Friends has been beyond measure. There were other areas needing specialist support. Adam Smith travelled into Leeds to comb sections of the Liddle Collection for suitable illustrative testimony on some of the less well-known aspects of the war and Albert Smith searched for men whose diaries and photographs enabled them to be used representatively to demonstrate the world-wide nature of the war in which Britons found themselves engaged. From the School of Geography, University of Leeds, David Appleyard worked on a format to express this cartographically and I thank him and his School for this assistance. Also from within the University of Leeds, Ann Pulleyn from the University Archives and Dr Tim Johnson from the Department of Animal Physiology and Nutrition directed me towards material of unusual interest and of which I had no knowledge.

For all this scholarly kindliness, I acknowledge a considerable debt. I would also like to thank Braham Myers and Hugh Cecil who have read and commented upon the text of the book and Carol Walder who has typed from a manuscript rendered legible only by familiarity with my scrawl during this last year during which she has been Secretary of the Leeds International 1914-18 Commemoration Week and Conference. I might add here that the organization of this September 1994 week of exhibitions, cultural, sporting and entertainment events and the four-day Conference has been the explanation of my being particularly needful of the voluntary support which I have outlined above. The other has been the move of the Collection from the Edward Boyle Library to the new Brotherton Library extension in the University. Locationally this is only a move of perhaps a little over three hundred yards. However, the two buildings concerned are quite separate and in terms of moving the evidence of more than six thousand sets of papers, of books, of tape-recordings, gramophone records, weapons, uniforms, newspapers, maps, posters, art work, midshipman sea chests and many items which are fragile or irregularly shaped, it was a challenging exercise.

While planning proceeded for both these events and the book, with its related exhibition took shape, other Friends of the Collection have maintained the normal work necessary to process documentation so that it is available for research. In this respect I would like to thank Keith and Brenda Clifton, Jacqueline Wynne Jones, Roy Venables, Muriel Booth, Molly Currie, Heather Taylor, Stuart Stott, Matthew Richardson, Barrie Herbert, Mike Hammerson, Daphne Estlick, Ian Joss, Kathleen Smith, Bill Lawson, Nobby Clark and Terry and Carolyn Mumford. A special note of appreciation must be added for Graham Stow acknowledging all that he has done successfully to promote the work of the Collection.

Institutionally I acknowledge gratefully the support of the University of Leeds and its Librarian, Reg Carr. In the regional archives consulted in Leeds, Bradford, Liverpool, Birkenhead, Glasgow, St Andrews, Dundee, Birmingham, Cardiff, Manchester, Durham, Sunderland, Newcastle, Chester-le-Street, Derby, Lincoln and Preston, staff were always sympathetic towards the nature of the enquiry put to them. Where photographs were selected the authorities were, without exception, helpful over the exercise of copyright reproduction and of course every photograph is credited appropriately. I would like to thank Anne Heap in Leeds, Susan Edwards in Cardiff, Nick Forder and Max Craven in Derby, Fergus Read in Nottingham, Andrew Davies in Lincoln, Naomi Evetts in Liverpool, Alan Bentley in Burton upon Trent, John Taylor with David Thomson in Birkenhead, Julie Harrop in Chester-le-Street, and staff at *The Herald*, Glasgow. I would like to pay special tribute to the trust offered in Derby, the way in which technology facilitated selection at Beamish, the North of England Open Air Museum, and to the sheer goodwill and efficiency at the Museum of Labour History in Manchester, the Museum of Lincolnshire Life in Lincoln (Lincolnshire County Council Leisure Services) and the Bass Brewers Limited Museum at Burton upon Trent. Malcolm Baxter in Grantham, with a fine private collection, has also been generous in his help and had it not been for the initiative of Dr Andrew Bamji, Director of Medical Education at the Frognal Centre of Medical Studies, Sidcup, I would not have known of the remarkable archive on facial reconstruction surgery in Sidcup. Similarly from Major J C M L Crawford of 'Combat Stress' I have learned of the case history documentation by the Ex-Services Welfare Society of its 70 years' support for victims of neurological disorder, an appropriately uncomfortable reminder to us of post-Armistice legacy which made home life difficult for some and for others asylum assimilation necessary.

Last but also first in everything, I thank my wife Louise and our children Felicity, Alexander and Duncan for the contentment of my home which allows the utmost challenge at work to be within reach.

Peter H Liddle, F.R.Hist.S. University of Leeds, January 1994

A note on the source of the illustrations: where a photograph has a personal name given as its source that photograph is in the Liddle Collection, the University Library, Leeds. The labels for all the other photographs give the name of the Institution or private collection from which that photograph was drawn.

Britons and their experience of the First World War

THE seminal significance of the First World War, common to all nations and peoples involved, is one explanation of the enduring interest in the 20th century's first global conflict. Central to there being no diminution of interest is a sort of 'wonderment' at the nature of the individual front line soldier's experience. That wonderment draws together sympathy, awe, outrage, incomprehension and, it must be said, admiration.

To us today the death or maiming of so many is a nightmare vision. Mercifully it is beyond anything within our experience. The dreadful toll of the Second World War, itself fearful to contemplate, is still appreciably less than half that scythed from the ranks of British soldiers in 1914-18. The scale can be demonstrated, though scarcely grasped, by the thought of not far short of the total population of a great city like Leeds at three-quarters of a million people, being obliterated. Such an example might be considered inapposite because of national statistics being regionally consolidated. We may, however, remind ourselves of the impact on communities when heavy losses were suffered by regionally recruited units like the Pals battalions from Northern towns. How many Newcastle upon Tyne or West Yorkshire or East Lancashire homes were blighted on one day in 1916?

The sense of loss at home is a second factor which exerts a sort of fascination rooted in an inability to comprehend what has to be recognized as fact. From thousands upon thousands of homes a central figure in the intimate world of a family had been permanently removed. Thoughts along such lines induce a need to identify who can be blamed for such a blight upon the nation. From 1919, with Germany to some considerable extent curiously protected by a British sense of guilt over the perceived injustice of the terms of the Treaty of Versailles, culpability had to become lodged nearer home. Post-war Britain offered enough reason for a sense of grievance. Inadequate pensions, unemployment, hunger, humiliation, unimproved living conditions were scarcely due reward for men who had undertaken active service in their country's declared need. Such a return encouraged the dispiriting onset of doubt as to the worthwhile nature of a man's service. Disillusionment thrived in dole, pension and job queues. At street corners, gatherings of the unemployed incubated the infection of resentment. Was this the victorious peace for which they had fought?

While sleek politicians in Government could be identified as blameworthy for the current circumstance, there was a growing body of public opinion convinced that the betrayal had begun earlier, before the war in the inequity of society,

during the war in military leadership by a class limited in all respects. Within this perception the limitation began with the narrowness of their social background, continued with an evaluation of their ability and their imagination and was conclusively concluded in the fruitless search for any evidence within them of human feelings for those whom they sent into battle.

By such a process the history of even recent events could be reshaped. New values lead to a reinterpretation of past experience. In the case of the First World War the process was accelerated in the 1930s by the publication of Lloyd George's memoirs so condemnatory of Haig and the High Command. In the 1960s the distortion was taken even further with the Generals as subjects for ridicule not just condemnation. Now, in the final decade of the twentieth century, historians are becoming uncomfortably aware that it is not just the intervening years which distance us from the immediacy of the 1914-18 experience, it is generations of changing ways of looking at things. 'Newly received wisdom' has altered or reinforced perceptions, has shaped judgements and cemented prejudices. So much for the rosy glow of distance lending enchantment.

If succeeding generations were to have made an unreasonable assessment of the way in which British troops were led in the First World War, what about the judgements handed down concerning the way the troops had responded to their experience and indeed how the nation as a whole had reacted to a prolonged trial?

Since the 1960s, in considering the Great War, we have been encouraged to focus upon war resistance, Red Clydeside, the stand of the Conscientious Objector, class differences in wartime hardship at home. On the fighting fronts, attention has been directed towards soldier disturbances and more recently upon the issue of Courts Martial and executions in the Field. In so doing what has been obscured is the remarkable national cohesion displayed in the waging of the war. Quite simply, without such cohesion the war could not have been won. There was certainly a gulf between Home Front experience and that of active service but as significant as this gulf was the effective operation of the interdependence between the worker and the serviceman.

Concerning women and the war, much attention has been paid to them in their response to the war and to the long-term significance of their temporarily widened employment and social opportunities but less to their being at the very heart of a people's national war effort.

The argument for a proper awareness of positive factors which emerge from an examination of the British war effort can be taken further, institutionally and in more human terms. Institutionally, the organization of the state's industrial and agricultural production, of its finances, of transport, of food supply and distribution, is worthy of approbation despite the errors which may be pointed out. Beneath the level of named management earning its accolades, there were numberless uncredited men and women whose work contributed to success. In the same way, households were run and work in a local community carried out by individuals known to few but who were sustaining the national endeavour by their undemonstrative personal resilience.

Of course most strikingly, that positive response to crisis was manifest through young men undertaking active service obligations. Similarly impressive was the whole range of voluntary supportive war work undertaken by women of all ages and men too young or too old for military service. It would be exceptionally difficult to estimate the percentage of the population responding by 'doing one's bit'. We would need to know how many Boy Scouts were watchful of the security of reservoirs and stretches of coastline, how many older men were undertaking Home Defence training, assisting with information for troops at railway stations or in some way with the reception or recuperation of wounded. Then there would be the men returning from retirement to resume work in business or industry left short of manpower by the surge to enlist. As for women, it would again be difficult to compute with any accuracy the numbers swiftly engaged in some form of war work. The sheer range of such work extends the imagination. It might include running a hostel for enemy aliens before they were interned, undertaking Belgian and then Serbian relief, nursing or driving cars and ambulances in France, Belgium and within the U.K., setting up and serving in canteens, billeting soldiers, labouring on the land. New charities were established and administered, their benevolent aim vigorously pursued. Girls searched for office vacancies, undertook heavy industry and munitions work, substitute labour of all kinds from road mending to coal delivery. They staffed information or relief agencies and, in small numbers, some organized and performed entertainment for the troops and for wounded whose welfare they succoured in other ways too. Then there was the making of comforts for the troops, scarves, balaclavas and body belts. Not all of this work was disinterested to be sure. There was money to be made in billeting soldiers. There were new opportunities for paid employment and, for the more financially secure, there was social credit to be gained in doing welfare work. There was a rewarding feeling of adventure and at the same time a sense of selfless mission.

There are further qualifying points to be made on all this endeavour though they do not invalidate the general picture. Many women lost employment in the dislocation of the economy caused by the war. Arthur Marwick points out with an acid touch of humour that when upper class ladies patriotically averted their thoughts from new dresses and fancy hats, they were helping to throw "almost half of the women occupied in the millinery, dressmaking and similar trades out of work or on short time". However, he also recognized that "probably the vast majority of women shared in the excitement and the quickening of the pulses engendered by the outbreak of the war"[1]. Certainly the picture has complexity. There are predictable differences in the area of voluntary effort given by people from different social backgrounds. The machinery of war may have chewed away at the structure upon which society was based but with some occupations the result would not be radical alteration. Some doors of opportunity were less open than others. Girls from varied backgrounds filled the ranks of the Women's Auxiliary Army Corps or the Women's Royal Naval Service, but the 1917 V.A.D. nurse was only marginally less likely to be of middle (or upper) class background than her counterpart in 1915.

In the overall picture, other points of check and balance which could be made would include the degree to which politically conscious women supported a war which was at first perceived as an interruption to their campaign rather than what it was to prove an opportunity. How superficial too was the unifying social effect of the emergency which covered the fissures 'in the body politic'? The pre-war sense of social injustice did not simply disappear, nor did the failure to resolve Irish problems. In retrospect it is easy to see these issues destined to emerge in a heated condition demanding priority consideration. It is, however, important to recognize that even under the prolonged strain of four and a half years of war, and in the case of Ireland a severe moment of testing, the unity which obscured the fault lines in British society had in fact its own dynamic. A reflection of that dynamic can be picked up in the opinions expressed and attitudes taken up by men and women living through the war. In original letters, diaries and photographs we can glimpse for our better understanding the interplay of action and reaction which carried Britons successfully through what was an unprecedented national trial. It is accordingly the individual's part in the context of a national effort which this book seeks photographically to document and to support this with the presentation of written or sketched personal experience testimony. What men and women made, or what weapons and technology they used in war, has been given a lower priority than showing people in their war locality, in their activity and the manner in which they responded to the challenge of war. Discordance with the national effort will be illustrated too and given its representative proportion.

A striking impression which should result from this approach will be the wide geographical stage on which Britons played their part. Pre-war regular soldiers and sailors had seen something of the world in the first years of the new century and enterprising souls (and perhaps some desperate souls too) had left the shores of the United Kingdom to make a new life in the Dominions and the United States. However, few workers in the workshop of the world in 1913 could have anticipated that as soldiers and at the expense of the Government they would soon see such far distant parts. It might be added sardonically that they would see much more besides and they might well not enjoy it nor live to recount the experience but nevertheless there is a major social point to be made. Young men whose physical horizons were limited to a small mill town in the Pennines, a mining community in the North East, one of the huge Midland or Northern drab conurbations, a village in Sussex, an isolated settlement in the Scottish Highlands or West Wales, might well find themselves in sight of the Rock of Gibraltar on a troopship bound for Alexandria. In due course they could be pitching tents in close proximity to the Pyramids. The Western Desert or the stark landscape of the Gaza Strip, the hills around Jerusalem, the humid climate of the Jordan Valley might then be their next new topographical experience. There is no denying that, whatever was to be said about the 'common soldiery', treading the pavements of Nazareth or Jerusalem was for some men a tremendous spiritual and cultural opportunity. From Alexandria further shipboard travel was possible, through the Suez Canal, with Aden and its oppressive heat, or Bombay with its Sub-Continent scents as a destination. For some there would have been alternative maritime routes to come next, around the Cape of Good Hope and after a South African halt, further voyage northwards to Mombasa. Campaigning from here inland could mean ascending the slopes of Mt Kilimanjaro, crossing tall grasslands inhabited by big game, or cutting trails through exceptionally dense vegetation.

The beautiful settings of land, water and sky in the maritime Middle East were within the appreciation of many in the Mediterranean Expeditionary Force even if it took a classical education to find inspiration in the nearness to Gallipoli of Troy and great deeds from a distant past. Mountains, marshy plains and lakes in Macedonia, Italy with her Alpine heights and the broad valley of the River Po, were to become familiar to many Britons. Some would endure the flood-changing flatness of Mesopotamia with its Old Testament associations, the mangrove-banked rivers of the Cameroons with its jungle vegetation. At the end of the war considerable numbers landed on the shores of the Kola Inlet in Northern Russia, coping with both mosquitoes and then snow and ice, being transported by barge up broad rivers bordered by mile upon mile of unrelieved forest. Campaigning in such circumstances stamps as incontestable the claim that the First World War widened the horizons of young men whose experience of foreign countries had hitherto lain at best in the imagination, at worst outside of consideration.

If we were to take specific examples, Douglas McIntyre, in 1914 just an office boy in a Newcastle spice importers firm, saw France and Belgium in 1917. In the same year, student Bill Mather of Sheffield served in Macedonia after troop train and troop ship journeys to Salonika via the South of France. In 1918, postman John Hammond of Oswestry reached Baghdad and Mosul after river steamers and motor transport had conveyed him from Basra through the ancient landscapes of the Fertile Crescent. Farm

labourer Harry Lowe of Tarporley voyaged to Alexandria, saw his first camels, transferred from the Cheshire Regiment into the Imperial Camel Corps and campaigned in Palestine. Jack Nicol, a coal merchant in Greenock, served on the Gallipoli Peninsula, (in fact losing a brother there) and later, still in the R.N.R. but no longer in the Royal Naval Division, was in North Atlantic Convoy work. More remote journeying still was undertaken by Rothkeale, County Limerick doctor, Norman Deane attached to the British West African Field Force in the Cameroons and by Albrighton, Shropshire doctor, James Elmsly Mitchell, who served in East Africa. Harold Blezard, a Burnley weaver, set off in 1918 for active service in North Russia but even the novelty of his travels was out-matched by Private Walter Hartley of Sudbury in Suffolk who journeyed to India and then, via Colombo and Hong Kong, to Vladivostok.

How did these men respond to such change? Foreign places, people and cultures, all newly experienced, must have stimulated a colourful confusion of mental impressions. Where these impressions were recorded in letters and diaries, what do they reveal about the uniformed Briton's reaction to the new course of his life? The first thing to be remarked is that it is the extraordinary difference in his life from all pre-war anticipation that had encouraged the keeping of a personal diary and the writing of letters. In the normal run of things he would have been unlikely to do either.

The second point to be made is that, while we can say from the examination of evidence that many men expressed an opinion along certain lines, this is not sufficient for the making of conclusive generalizations. In quoting the opinion of an individual on some matter of general interest, it has to be recognized of course that this is simply one man's viewpoint at the moment of writing. The man may well change his views; the circumstances which led him to write as he did may have been very particular. It would be surprising if those circumstances were to have been fully shared by all those who expressed judgement on the same subject. After these considerations, we might also raise the question of the social and educational background of the writer, his character and temperament too.

There are other qualifications which might be levelled at any generalization based on insufficiently large samples of comparable testimony. To what extent is the letter writer influenced by Army Censorship or by feelings for the person to whom the letter is addressed? Furthermore, a case could be made for examination of the motives of a diarist in writing his diary and a consideration of how that may have influenced the opinions he expressed. Of course diaries can be merely 'a record'. Such a record can be for self, for family in due course or for an aide memoire in future recall of days currently recognized as having left far behind the ordinariness of office or factory routine. (This having been noted, a diary would reveal a new routine, that of life in the Army!)

In ready acknowledgement that generalization from opinions expressed in personal letters is potentially flawed,

9

it is still thought-provoking to look at judgements which fall within the mainstream of opinion on topics central to the soldier in the line. It is thought-provoking not least by reason of the contrast between the evidence and 'received wisdom' on the lines of 'well we all know what the First World War soldier felt about his experience'.

We might look first at what the British soldier in France wrote of his German foe. Selecting evidence from a later period than 1914 and 1915 where views might well be more immediately conditioned by stories of atrocities or one-sided interpretations of what became international incidents like the sinking of the *Lusitania* or the execution of Edith Cavell, we find men referring in 1917 to the Germans as 'absolute swine'[2] and looking like 'vile and brute beasts'[3]. 'I have had the most complete satisfaction of killing some Germans myself. I feel ever so pleased'[4] was the way one expressed his views. Another wanted to know 'if the new Tank photos in the Press show the swines being squashed to jelly ... how I hate the huns.'[5] These sentiments seem to last out the war and beyond. Faced with duties in the Army of Occupation in December 1918, a letter records, 'I was not keen on going to Germany. I have seen all I want to see of the Hun and his ways'[6]. One who did serve in the Rhineland made an observation which was by no means unparalleled: 'The streets are full of boys who I suppose will grow up to try and conquer the world again.'[7]

In truth when one looks for evidence among ordinary soldiers for any identification with German soldiers as men locked unfortunately together in a struggle not of their making, it is thin on the ground. There are some acknowledgements of 'jolly decent Saxons'[8], of 'gentle and considerate German stretcher bearers'[9] and subsequent medical treatment of wounded British P.O.W.s but it is the martial qualities of the German nation, the fighting efficiency of its front-line soldiers, the quality of his equipment which earn almost exclusively whatever contemporary tribute to the Germans is paid in British wartime letters or diaries. 'The Germans are hard men to down; [it] will take discipline and all our effort'; '[there is] no sign of the end; the Germans seem able to fight the whole world'[10], and 'we are not fighting an ordinary nation, we are fighting a nation of the most wonderful organization and discipline as has ever existed or will exist'.[11]

From soldier opinion of his foe to the soldier's view of a war extending into a fourth year and beyond, would seem a reasonable progression. Thoughts on the war as such would certainly be within his consideration though not a constant preoccupation. Such centrality was reserved for matters immediately affecting him; food, cold, wetness, responsibilities and his standing with his comrades. However, the act of writing a letter home, bringing loved ones to the forefront of consciousness, also stimulated reflections on how the writer was coping with the war. There is a wealth of impressive testimony of men awaiting an ordeal like a major battle, writing of their patriotic conviction that British ideals had to be upheld at whatever cost. 'Keep smiling. I am more than pleased that I have at last been given the opportunity to fight for my King and Country. I only hope I may be fearless and shall fight in such a way that you will feel proud of your son,' wrote W. J. Palk in July, 1916[12]. Charlie Bosher on the eve of the Battle of Loos in September of the previous year recognized that 'it is almost certain that a lot of us will go under and in case it should fall to my lot to be one of them ... I for one am well content if by my death our righteous cause is aided by the merest fraction'[13]. It was to be poor Bosher's lot to die, but, from the noble sentiments of men writing without insight of the ordeal they might face, we should look at the statements of men who had experienced or were going through a prolonged period of active service in France.

Raymond Charlesworth admitted in a 1918 letter that the 'nearer and fuller acquaintance with real war has not affected me as much as I had expected'[14]. As surprisingly, W. A. Rigden found his 'fear replaced by boredom'[15] and G. E. Raven wrote of a 1917 battle that 'I wouldn't have missed it for anything but I am quite glad it is over'[16]. We cannot ask him why he wouldn't have missed it for anything but ironically it is in such terms that many veterans have written retrospectively of a war service which in all likelihood was harshly demanding of their bodies and spirit.

There is abundant evidence of stoic acceptance of what was required of a man as the war was extended into 1917 and 1918 but there is also evidence of a more cheerful resilience. T. E. H. Helby considered a December, 1917, day in the Ypres Salient 'one of the best days of my life'[17] and in the previous month a soldier, known from his letter simply as 'Alf', told his parents to ignore the gloom in the papers, he was confident victory would be won.[18] Harry Old, clearly a contemplative soul, saw that for secular salvation 'the road to the Utopian ideal lies as surely along these earth-lined communication trenches as along the golden path of art and literature'[19].

Arnold Hooper, in his 1918 letters, regularly showed a positive response to his trials. In January 'We must be the better for all this business ... we have had our corners knocked off'. Five months later he was 'just beginning to think that four years is enough of most things even of jolly old wars', but his spirits, if they were at all depressed, revived in the following month: 'What a wonderful war this is. By Jove I am proud of our British Empire'[20]. J. C. Hold, when admitting that he was 'longing for his ticket' (to get home) added 'but if there's a chance of a V.C. I'm going to have a try'[21].

Because the evidence is so unfamiliar in its tone, so foreign to our preconceptions, it is all the more important that it should give pause for reflection. J. D. Urquhart believed that active service for him in France was 'a great, a glorious, a romantic and adventurous life and we are fighting for civilization'[22]. He was echoing sentiments expressed by A. S. G. Butler: 'Life out here is a very wonderful thing. People are seen at their best'[23], and Gilbert Verity declared that he would 'be glad of this experience if one comes through'[24].

There is testimony in support of L. D. Fairfield's weariness as he wondered 'whether I would ever live to play with children of my own in a peaceful country – never have I longed for peace and quiet, a wife and a home of my own so much'[25], and anxiously Army authorities scrutinized mail for signs of any weakening of resolve. This very fact draws attention to the likely inhibitions upon the expression of disillusionment in communications going through the Army Postal Service and even if it must be recognized that an unknown number of men may have felt what J. B. Herbert expressed in 1918 letters, an utter loathing for the war and its foul destruction, examination today of what remains of 1917/1918 British soldier correspondence shows morale holding up well. Herbert had summarily rejected the ideals which had inspired men to enlist and which some still openly espoused. He felt that he was a conscript to 'the good opinions of my neighbours' and that the war was being prolonged by 'old men's dead and rotting minds and by the folly of the mob'[26]. Beside the vehemence of his opinions should be set the fact that this subaltern fulfilled his responsibilities and received recognition for his work in the form of a Military Cross award.

Trevor Wilson, who has written what many would judge to be the best general study of Britain in the First World War, chose well in entitling his book *The Myriad Faces of War*. It points us in the right direction, away from simple generalization and towards individual variation even in that same individual. Within that proper caution, it is reasonable to look at the soldiering test faced by Britons opposed to Germans and their redoubtable allies, to look at the expressed views of officers and men enduring that test before the national outcome was known and then look at the outcome itself. It is not then an over-simplified generalization to conclude that a national achievement built upon individual achievement is there for all to see. Wilson judged that in the culminating process of beating her adversary, 'Britain played a large and even predominant part'. He was writing of the Western Front ('Haig's armies drove their enemies from one stronghold to another') but he might well have drawn the wider war into his verdict. There too his words would have been as apposite.[27]

While no one would doubt that the role of the sailor and airman was essential to that national achievement, what needs re-emphasis is the fundamental part played by women in the war effort. In practical and in emotional terms, in collective and in individual effort, in factory and in home, in uniform of all kinds and in an apron, the strain was taken and held.

There is rich documentation for this, but it is uneven, rich in photographs and in the keeping of diaries and autograph albums by middle class girls, less ample in terms of letters. Women serving abroad as V.A.D. nurses, or in the First Aid Nursing Yeomanry or as W.A.A.C.s assuredly wrote letters home to the U.K. with a goodly number surviving. However, soldiers overseas receiving letters, despite the importance the letters held, did not keep them in the way their own letters were treasured by the recipient at home. Of course it was far less easy so to do. Fortunately sufficient letters from loving mothers, sisters, wives and girlfriends do survive and they speak eloquently of wartime circumstance. There is supportive concern for a man's welfare, his needs and what can be posted out for his comfort. Then there is the picture of domestic trivia bringing home nearer to the reader changes at father's office, a younger sister's birthday, Aunt Hilda's health, the prices of commodities, the lameness of the dog, 'doings' at the church or chapel and then, by statement or implication, the heartache of separation and thinly disguised anxiety for the soldier's safety.

Much less well documented by surviving letters or diaries is the daily working life of a munitions girl. Her life can be pictured from photographs, from other people's observations or official reports on her work and from recollections she was encouraged to make at a later period of her life. Mrs Nina Cooper clearly remembered her 1916 work at the large munitions factory at Gretna, north of Carlisle. 'We lived in hostels, just wooden huts with long dormitories and a large living room with wooden forms to sit on and a big iron stove (no comforts). Each girl had a small bedroom, no door just curtain at the doorway, and it was very cold in the cold weather; as the maids washed the floors they turned to ice as they dried out. Each hostel had a name, mine was 'Flora McDonald'. We worked in three shifts and we went to work in trains with wooden seats and each one of us had a pass to show before we were allowed in the large gates. We made cordite. We changed into overalls and hats to cover all our hair and shoes that must not touch the ground outside of where we worked. We made the cordite, cut it in lengths, packed it in trays and then carried it to small trucks at the doorway and two girls pushed the truck a mile or so to large stoves where it was dried out. It was an awful job when on the trucks if on nightshift – cold, rain, dark and lonely pushing the heavy trucks and rats running round your feet. Sometimes the girls were drunk with fumes from the cordite and had to be taken to the sick bay to sleep it off. Dinner was served always cold but we ate it as we were always hungry. There was a hall in the village where we could go at weekends and dance with boys who came in from Carlisle. There was a medical hut where we had to go about once a month to have our hair combed with a small tooth comb to keep our heads clean. We earned about two to three pounds per week with thirteen shillings deducted for board and lodging.'[28]

Air raids inspired detailed description, of course. One over Pontefract in November, 1916, was described by V.A.D. Nurse Flora Evans as 'most thrilling'. After bombs had been dropped nearby, the raid seemed over and 'we all calmed down again' but the raider returned, dropping bombs on the town itself. 'It shook this house very much and made an awful noise. We could see flashes and hear the engines all the time ... I was attired in a dressing gown and coat and an eiderdown.'[29] Intriguingly, Home Front accounts of air raids gave rise to a split response in soldiers' letters. On the one hand, some soldiers from their vantage point made light of the raids: there was little to fear from them and as long as they were not endangering the family home they would have the good effect of enlightening 'slackers' or the comfortably secure at home that there really was a war on. The second reaction, one expressed by sufficient men for it to be mentioned, is an utter contempt and fury towards the Germans that they should endanger civilians at home. Of course such views disregard British bombing of German towns but war is not a time for balanced views.

Women were not left to consider that they might have a part to play, they were told that their struggle is 'in your larder, your kitchen and your dining room. Every meal you serve is literally a battle. Every well cooked meal that saves bread and wastes no food is a victory'[30]. Such stern admonitions were followed up with recipes for stewed nettles and fish sausages.

Largely under the care of women were the nation's children and, while some children actually fell victim to the enemy raids from sea or sky, few wholly escaped the impact of the war. Eleven year old Kitty Alexander's diary recorded: 'Bab's father is killed. I am very sorry but of course she must be very proud of him'. This was in November, 1915, and at the end of the war she was writing: 'The Germans are whining now because they want us to feed them but after the way they've sent our prisoners back it's not likely we will show any mercy'[31].

A teenage girl working in a photographer's shop in Kirkwall in the Orkneys kept her diary throughout the war. On 3 June, 1916, she wrote: 'Rumours were afloat that a naval engagement was going on on Wednesday 31 May but I could not believe it true. Last night Jim and I worked until 11pm putting new glass in a large picture of one of our Fleet men on the *Bellerophon* when Maggie came in and told us a battle had really taken place and ten of our ships were sunk. After that I could do no more work for thinking of all our men who had pictures in to be framed and who, poor souls, might never come back ... all day the territorials were burying the dead at Longhope so we were told. What a gloom was cast over the town and how depressed we all were to think of our noble ships and brave sailors and officers going down.' In April, 1918, this girl wrote of a rumoured raid on the Orkneys and posters being put up warning people to leave their homes without delay and go into the country if there were to be a bombardment. 'I expect I shall be very frightened if they do really come but I am not in the least nervous yet.'[32]

That the three women in a comfortably off family in Cambridge took the war very seriously is made abundantly clear in their letters and diaries. With one brother wounded and another who would be invalided out of the army with serious malaria complications, twin girls Betty and Molly Macleod engaged upon various forms of voluntary war work from potato lifting, harvesting flax to V.A.D. nursing. They also undertook teacher training courses which

themselves reflected the impact of the war. Their brothers were kept supplied with food parcels and lionized on their leaves. On 21 May, 1915, Jock Macleod came home on leave looking 'tired and white'. On 6 June, Rory was briefly in Cambridge. 'He told us he had been fighting at Festubert. He looks very sunburned.' Two days later Betty took a First Aid exam, passed and was accepted by Miss Bishop's Voluntary Aid Detachment Convalescent Home (Huntly). On 19 August she began work: 'Stained a floor, cleaned out office including washing shelves, black leading grate, sweeping and scrubbing floor.' The first patients arrived on 22 September and Betty received her official title 'Extra Nursing Orderly'.

In 1917 Molly Macleod went potato lifting near Guildford. 'You feel very "worky" whilst at it but chucking lime on the heaps of taties gives you the flu.' In the same year Mrs Macleod had her son Jock home as an invalid but rationing recommendations [before rationing became mandatory in 1918] made her 'fearfully troubled' because 'I would like of course to give him everything nice and yet how can one do so and stick to the rations?'[33].

The constant possibility of the loss of a son or a husband must itself have been an anxiety only dispelled by fierce deliberate 'busyness'. Not infrequently when bereavement struck, such was the local or regimental scale of the tragedy that the burden was collectively borne. Replying to a letter of condolence from the wife of a Commanding Officer, the latter having been killed too, Grace Addams-Williams wrote that 'your beautiful letter has just come and that has done me more good than I can tell you. To think you could find time to write to me, in the midst of your own grief, makes me feel how selfish I have been.... Our boy was the light of our life and had been nothing but a pure joy from the day of his birth. He was always so happy and good-tempered and unselfish and the thought of the future without him is unspeakable'[34].

From a less privileged background, the loving message of a young wife, Emily Meredith, offers some indication of what would be the extent of her grief when she lost her husband Tom. 'Dear Loving Husband, Received your letter this morning. Not much news love however don't be afraid I shall not forget you for it made me think of you knowing that you would like a baby. How do you like the P.C. [picture of a soldier embracing his girl] I wish it was me in your arms. .... Don't forget to get on to them [about leave?] Don't leave it a long time or you will never get. I am not neglecting you if it is only a card, you're my loving husband, your loving wife Emily'[35].

When inconclusive information was received concerning a man being wounded and with no further details yet available or of his being posted missing, the strain of uncertainty must have been severe. Annie Tait of Ashington, Northumberland, received such a letter and, despite all likelihood, kept the faint flickering of hope even into the postwar years. Lance Corporal Tait's body was never found. He was hit at Suvla on the Gallipoli Peninsula in August, 1915, and was reported as wounded. Evidence to corroborate the presumption that he had been killed was elicited from Red Cross enquiries but when Mrs Tait learned in March, 1916, from the secretary of the Lord Mayor of Newcastle's War Information Office that such evidence left 'little room for hope that your husband is still alive' it was still not something which she could accept without irrefutable proof.[36]

Grief, coming to terms with loss, spiritual consolation, are matters to which Dr J. M. Winter has recently given academic consideration.[37] Related to this whole question is the impact the war had on spinsterhood in the 1920s and beyond. Recognizing of course that an unknown number of women would in any case have chosen that status, for how many of the rest who remained spinsters was it a question of a shortage of supply of eligible males and for how many an aching void which could not be filled? We are never going to know the answer to that question but in the last thirty years I have received from a number of spinsters bundles of ribbon-tied letters from their fiancés who did not return from France. I have also received a small notebook of poems and private thoughts written by one grieving young woman. On Armistice day her despair was expressed in a tirade of personal and national betrayal:

'So it has come? the day when this war which has wrecked my life and altered my whole character, and what does it mean to us? Us − who have lost our all in this fight? a fight which is not won, it is wickedly unfair to our dead, you dear boy are the only one I think of, of course but very soon will England have to answer for this base piece of treachery in which many millions of brave lads like yourself went 'West' only to have been sold as the English Government would sell anybody and anything. But England's day is over, the Throne shakes, Ireland openly hates England and will soon be out of their power, Scotland silently hates the English and is working swiftly but steadily for the time when they will be free also. France, Italy and all other 'allied' countries turn away from England to America, the country which will in a few years head the world. How America despises England, which pretends to be so clever and with her bad ruling, petty strikes and pigheadedness is losing trade and every other thing which makes a country famous.

'And here − on this night when all are laughing and enjoying themselves left alone I sit and think of what it might have been like had not you been taken away and my heart were not slowly breaking. This night when 'everyone is happy' as people say, Dear Lord! have mercy it is not in human nature to stand so much.'

There is no need critically to examine the logic of her broader views; one hopes that time would ease her pain but at the end of October, 1922, more than four years after the loss of her fiancé, Lt Philip Pemble R.A.F., she wrote:

'Even if one lives to be a hundred and married sixty times and had twice as many children I don't think it would make any difference to one hurt or the old

ache which somehow always manages to be as sharp as a surgeon's knife even though it sometimes remains dulled for a few days but always it crops up again with its death-dealing feeling until it has killed every little tiny joy that there might be.'[38]

In this introduction I have been concerned to write principally about soldiers and women, each within defined limitations. In the case of the soldiers it was simply about the way they viewed their German foes and about a war lasting well beyond expectation. In the case of women it was about their coping emotionally and to some extent practically with the challenges and crises brought by war. This has meant that maritime or air experience has been untouched and only tangential reference has been made to the industrial scene where, quite literally, millions of people were employed and where the part played by women was fundamental. Soldier and civilian captivity has been neglected; there has been little reference, beyond the mention of location, to campaigning overseas and not much to the actual conditions in France under which the line was held or offensives undertaken. War Resistance has been similarly passed over in the text. The decision for all of this has been quite deliberate: this is a picture book and all of these topics will be represented by photographs or other forms of documentation.

The first section of the book includes pictorial evidence of pre-war society and then of the actual outbreak of war, the first soldiering in Belgium and France while New Armies were being created and the Empire was responding with support. The second section looks at the threat and the opportunity of war in the air, the Dardanelles Gallipoli campaign, the maritime challenge and soldiering in distant lands.

The third area to be covered is the Home Front in the heart of the war. The industrial scene, women and children in wartime, fund raising and voluntary endeavour, food economy and rationing, strikes, war resistance and conscientious objection and the Dublin Easter Rebellion are represented in this section. The fourth and final part of the book deals with British soldier and civilian captivity, soldiering on the Western Front from the Somme to the end and then images of the Armistice and beyond.

Where it seems appropriate, the original captions on photographs are incorporated in labels in order to retain the personal intimacy of the albums from which the selection was made. Herein lies one element in the challenge of the book, the attempt sharply to focus on men, women and children as individuals but also as representatives of the unseen Britons each engaged upon his or her own First World War.

NOTES

1. Arthur Marwick *Women at War 1914-18* Fontana 1977, p 34.
2. W Norrie, Liddle Collection, University of Leeds
3. B H Puckle, Liddle Collection, University of Leeds
4. R J W Ledingham, Liddle Collection, University of Leeds
5. E G Bates, Liddle Collection, University of Leeds

6. E A Smith (A & C Black papers) Liddle Collection, University of Leeds

7. E P Neville, Liddle Collection, University of Leeds

8. H E Hopthrow, Liddle Collection, University of Leeds

9. H B Lyon, Liddle Collection, University of Leeds

10. J M MacLachlan, Liddle Collection, University of Leeds

11. L F S Sotheby, Liddle Collection, University of Leeds

12. W J Palk, Liddle Collection, University of Leeds

13. Charlie Bosher letter, Liddle Collection, University of Leeds

14. R Charlesworth, Liddle Collection, University of Leeds

15. W A Rigden, Liddle Collection, University of Leeds

16. G E Raven, Liddle Collection, University of Leeds

17. T E H Helby, Liddle Collection, University of Leeds

18. 'Alf', Liddle Collection, University of Leeds

19. Harry Old, Liddle Collection, University of Leeds

20. Arnold Hooper, Liddle Collection, University of Leeds

21. J C Hold, Liddle Collection, University of Leeds

22. J D Urquhart, Liddle Collection, University of Leeds

23. A S G Butler, Liddle Collection, University of Leeds

24. G Verity, Liddle Collection, University of Leeds

25. L D Fairfield, Liddle Collection, University of Leeds

26. J B Herbert, Liddle Collection, University of Leeds

27. Trevor Wilson, *The Myriad Faces of War,* Polity Press, Cambridge, 1986, p 584-5

28. Mrs Nina Cooper, Liddle Collection, University of Leeds

29. Miss Flora Evans, Liddle Collection, University of Leeds

30. From *The Win the War Cookery Book* Liddle Collection, University of Leeds

31. Miss Kitty Alexander, Liddle Collection, University of Leeds

32. Jean, later Mrs J Robb, Liddle Collection, University of Leeds

33. Mrs E M, Miss E and Miss M L Macleod Liddle Collection, University of Leeds

34. J Napier, Liddle Collection, University of Leeds

35. Mr and Mrs T Meredith, Liddle Collection, University of Leeds

36. Mrs A Tait, Liddle Collection, University of Leeds

37. J M Winter, *Wartime Spiritualism in France, Britain and Germany* Paper given at Trinity College, Dublin, 24 June 1993

38. Phyllis Constance Iliff, Liddle Collection, University of Leeds

Opposite: Built at Cammell Lairds, HMS *Audacious*, a new Dreadnought battleship enters No 7 Dock at the Birkenhead yard on the Mersey. For all her majesty symbolizing one area at least where Britain appeared ready for war, she was to be the first and only British Dreadnought lost at sea, in October, 1914, to a mine.

Cammell Laird Archives: Wirral County Council

EARLY DAYS

Eve and Outbreak
The Call to Arms
The British Expeditionary Force in France and Belgium
The Response of Empire

Opposite above: Women and children gathering coal from slag during the 1912 coal strike.

National Museum of Labour History, Manchester

Opposite below: Working class living conditions, Flowerpot Yard, King Street, Derby in 1913.

Derby Museum

Below: Working class living conditions, Burlington Street, Liverpool 1914

Liverpool Libraries and Museum Service

Opposite above: Suffragists on a demonstration march from Edinburgh to London pass through Grantham, Lincolnshire on 5 November, 1912. They are led by Mrs de Fonblanque. Interviewed by the *Grantham Journal*, the women conveyed to the reporter an 'impression of their intense earnestness of conviction'. They had marched, on one occasion, almost thirty miles in a day!

Malcolm Baxter Collection, Grantham

Opposite below: Helping with the hay.

Miss Kitty Alexander

Right: Summer holiday, 1914. The Manse, Kenmore, Tayside, Scotland: 'Ida, Dorothy, "Doff", Margie Nicol, Christian.'

P Haig Ferguson

Below: Dr Alexander of Broadway takes one of his sons and his daughter Kitty for a picnic.

Miss Kitty Alexander

Opposite above: Schoolboys at peace on the eve of being officers at war. Truro College senior boys, H.C. Rickard, A.E. Tregea and F.E. Gilpin, Malpas, Truro in 1914.

F E Gilpin

Opposite below: Crowds around the notice of mobilization for war, Reading Town Hall, August, 1914.

Reading County Reference Library

Above: Mobilization for war, August 1914, Rothesay: The Rothesay Battery, 4 Highland Mountain Artillery Brigade.

J Lindsay Smith

Right: 'This beastly war!' With war imminent, a schoolboy writes home from Shrewsbury School's Officer Training Corps camp.

Y Kirkpatrick

SHREWSBURY
O.T.C.

O.T.C. CAMP,
HAGLEY PARK,
RUGELEY.

August 2. 1914.

Dear Mother

Thank you very much for your letters. I shall probably arrive on Thursday at 9 at about 5.15 P.M. That is of course if all goes well, but one does not know where we will be next Thursday with this beastly war. There are rumours that the camp will

Above: Seaplane readiness, July, 1914, Isle of Grain, near Sheerness.

P Haig Ferguson

Left, opposite, and over page: Inventions to win the war: A pilotless torpedo aircraft and a vertical take-off aircraft put forward on 16 August, 1914, by Motor and Cycle Engineer, F.W. Rosser. Official response was: 'One must try to keep to ideas that can be made use of at once.'

F W Rosser

16 Aug/14 190

M .... The Adjutant, Royal Flying Corps

~~Bought of~~ **F. W. ROSSER,**

From

Motor and Cycle Engineer,

97, WHYTEVILLE ROAD, FOREST GATE, LONDON, E.

Dear Sir,
            am enclosing particulars
of two ideas which may be of
great use to the Nation in this
critical crisis.
    Shall esteem it a great favour
if you will carefully peruse same,
& any further assistance I can
supply, shall be most pleased to
place at your disposal.
        Of course many items must
of necessity be omitted from
such short discription of two
ideas of this kind.
    awaiting the favor of an early com-
munication & trusting that ideas

97 Whytevilla Rd, Forest Gate London E

1.4.

16 August 1914

Torpedo Aeroplanes

Would suggest that small aeroplanes capable of carrying pilot only could be used for purpose above stated; pilot would, of course, not be carried, a heavily charged torpedo being substituted.

The aeroplane would be driven by the usual type of motor, elect- electrically controlled to run for any stated period according to the range that was found by ex- perience to be most effective.

Planes, steering gear, &c would be locked in required position to make aeroplane follow as nearly as possible the line of flight taken by shells fired from ordinary large guns; an alternate method ~~could would~~ would be for flight of aeroplane to finish at any height desired & then fall vertically

This course would probably have this objection, the aeroplane being

[illegible]

3. 16 August 1914

Improved Aeroplane.

In this short article I wish to briefly describe a plan whereby aeroplanes can be made to start & alight vertically (no run required), and also hover in any position, two great advantages not possessed to the best of my knowledge by any present type of aeroplane.

To achieve the above a motor more on the lines of the ordinary automobile type would have to be used, or present pattern of aeroplane engine altered slightly.

Main shaft would be required to extend backward as well as forward to propellor, & counter-shaft driven either by bevel gear, or suitable gearbox to which vertical propellor would be fitted; said shaft & propellor being so fitted than when not required for ascending, alighting, or hovering could be swung forward, & so

Above: 4th Battalion Essex Regiment in full kit and marching order.   *E Abrams*

Above: New 'Gentlemen Cadets' at Woolwich in 1914. (F.E. Gilpin indicated with
an arrow).   *F E Gilpin*

Opposite above: 4th Battalion Essex Regiment at Drayton Camp; protection for
all and a test for some – the mandatory inoculation.   *E Abrams*

Opposite below: From the same Territorial unit; commercial enterprise and a badge
of manliness – backstreet tattooist at work.   *E Abrams*

Below: 4th Battalion Essex Regiment cooks at Drayton Camp in 1915. *E Abrams*

Above: 'Put your hand out you naughty boy'. Essex Territorials; the 4th Battalion Essex Regiment recruits submit to an inspection of hands.   *E Abrams*

Opposite above: Where do we go from here? (Essex Territorials).   *E Abrams*

Opposite below: Middleton-in-Teesdale sends off a Territorial.
                                        Beamish: The North of England Open Air Museum

Below: Best feet forward for inspection. (Essex Territorials).   *E Abrams*

AND AT 21, MINCING LANE, LONDON, E.C.

Telegraphic Address:
"EKOOR, LIVERPOOL".

Telephone Nº 1308 CENTRAL.

HENRY ROOKE, SONS & CO,
DYEWOOD & GENERAL BROKERS.

SOLE AGENTS IN THE UNITED KINGDOM FOR
THE SALE OF THE
OLEIFICI NAZIONALI
"CASTLE BRAND" GREEN OLIVE OIL SOAP.

ALSO
AGENTS FOR
JOHN H. HEALD & CO
(LYNCHBURG-VIRGINIA, U.S.A.)
QUERCITRON EXTRACT, PASTE & SOLID,
OAKWOOD EXTRACT,
SUMAC EXTRACT.

22 & 23, Irwell Chambers East,
FAZAKERLEY STREET,
Liverpool, August 6th 1914   19

My dear old Lal,

I now understand that you leave the old country for foreign service to Egypt.

I shall not be able to come up to town to see you off owing to the terrible dislocation of business here.

I can only therefore repeat that I am proud of my sons fighting for their country, wives and sweethearts.

I wish you all success, and that the "Flag of England" will still continue to rule the world.

If we never meet again remember the last and fondest wish of your loving father is "God bless you," and, in due course, may you return to England crowned with victory.

With the heartiest of hand grips,

I remain,

Your loving father,

Louis F. Rooke

Above: Leeds University Officer Cadets undergo signalling
training near Bolton Abbey in Wharfedale.
Leeds University Archives

Right: Academically correct: A Leeds University Officer
Cadet in training.   *Leeds University Archives*

Opposite: 'I am proud of my sons fighting for their country,
wives and sweethearts.' A father bids farewell to the first of
his boys. He was to lose two and the third was to be badly
injured.   *The Rooke family*

Below: Cammell Laird Territorials drill in No 6 dock at their
shipyard, 13 August,1914.
Cammell Laird Archive: Wirral County Council

In Grateful Memory.

THE YORKSHIRE ELEVEN.

NOTE—The first List of Dead from the Front contained the names of the following eleven Officers of the King's Own Yorkshire Light Infantry :—

Colonel Bond.
Major Yate.
Captains Ackroyd, Gatacre, Keppel and Luther.
Lieutenants Denison, Rawdon and Wynne.
Second Lieutenants Noel and Ritchie.

No Football Team is here! Not Cricket, this!
No "Soccer" Cup, with shining "Barnsley Brights"
No record Bowling Game of Doughty Drake—
But Players in War's International!
Our King's Own Yorkshires! Gone at one fell swoop!
Yet gone so gloriously we scarce can grieve.
Brave Band of Brothers! Leaders of the Team
Our County sent to join the New Crusade!
Upon War's Fatal Field the first to fall,
Ye, on our Roll of Fame, the last shall stay !—
Our Dauntless Dead who Died at Duty's call!
Who fought to win your Land a lasting Peace!
We dare not mourn you! Rest ye Noble Souls!
You fell for Friends! For Freedom! For the Right!
Ye Martyrs who redeemed your Country's Bond!
Whose hero-blood her debt of honour paid—
Her children yet unborn shall bless your names—
Shall honour, too, each soldier whom you led.

WANDERING TYKE.

September 5th, 1914.

Above: The hallowed turf of Cardiff Arms Park put to
emergency use for the training of Royal Engineer recruits.
Cardiff Yesterday No 16 and Miss I Jenkins

Right: 'You 'orrible little man!'- an autograph album memory.
Annie Storey

Opposite: A sporting tribute in verse to eleven officers of the
King's Own Yorkshire Light Infantry killed in the earliest
fighting in Belgium and France.   *Leeds City Libraries*

Below: Volunteers parade in Mitchell and Butlers Brewery
Yard, Cape Hill, Birmingham.   *Bass Museum, Burton upon Trent*

BUSINESS MEN

SHOW YOUR PATRIOTISM.

Your Country Needs YOU

HER PERIL IS GREAT

JOIN THE

LEEDS CITY
BATTALION

(Age Limit 19 to 35)

Register yourselves at the

TOWN HALL, LEEDS

Open Daily: 9 a.m. to 9 p.m.

Your friends are joining

WHY NOT YOU?

E. A. BROTHERTON, Lord Mayor.

ALF COOKE, LTD., Printers, LEEDS AND LONDON.

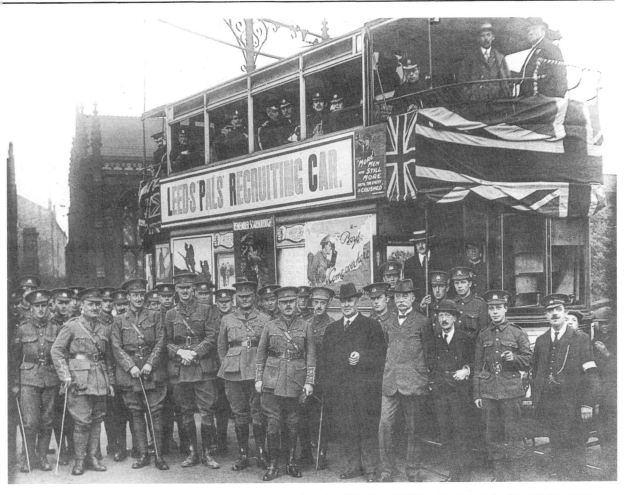

Above: Recruiting by tram car for the Leeds Pals, June, 1915: This photograph shows the following officers from left to right, Smith, Anderson, Whittaker and Major Howard. In the middle stands Lt Colonel S.C. Taylor with Capt Bathurst between Taylor and the first civilian, J.B. Hamilton. The next civilian is J. Wardle while Dr White to the right fingers his watch chain.
Leeds City Libraries

Opposite: The Lord Mayor of Leeds appeals for recruits from the business community for the Leeds Pals.
Leeds City Libraries

Right: An inventor brings to Leeds University Officer Cadet Squadron his device for blowing away enemy barbed wire.
Leeds University Archives

Above: Bass and Company brewers' wagons and horses, now 'transport' for the 6th
Battalion, North Staffordshire Regiment.   *Bass Museum, Burton upon Trent (86.0997.00)*

Below: 'The Babykillers Raid', Hartlepool, Whitby and Scarborough, victims of
German shelling, 16 December, 1914. Prospect Road, Scarborough is shown here;
the shopkeeper's wife was killed at her door. Posters were to use this raid to stimulate
recruitment and fortify resolve on the Home Front. Figures issued at the time put the
casualty toll at 78 dead and 228 injured.   *Liddle Collection*

Above: 4.5 inch howitzer ready for action.
K W Brewster

Opposite above: Rest on the retreat from Mons. 11 am 25 August, 1914, and the men of the 1st Battalion Cameronians have been walking since 3 am when they left Mons. A German plane had been observing them since daylight and an officer (Vandeleur) is now watching it observe their rest.
R C Money

Opposite below: Still retreating: 29 August, 1914, and the Cameronians, having arrived at Pontoise at 2 am stir themselves for breakfast and whatever the day may hold.
R C Money

Right: 1 September, 1914, and the retirement continues: French cavalry 'with glittering breastplates and helmets' and the wreckage of L Battery RFA at Nery.
E M Lyons

Below: 1 September, 1914, and the Queen's Bays with some captured German Cavalry (Death's Head Hussars) after the 'L Battery affair at Nery'.
R C Money

On our way across the plain to Nery my mind went back to stories of the Napoleonic wars, as there were groups of French Cuirassier complete with their glittering Breastplate & Helmets taking cover behind several haystacks, a most unsuitable dress in War. As we got near the Village most distressing sights met us. On the roadside there were turned over limbers complete with teams of poor horses all killed trying to escape and just off the roadside were lying the bodies of the drivers. I felt very sad. In the Village I assisted the RAMC men to load up the Ambulances. After the last one went off full up I was still scouting around to make sure there were no more Wounded. There was one we couldn't get in the Ambulance he was so badly wounded so we borrowed a farm cart and packed it with straw and made him as comfortable as possible. He was the 'L Battery' Commander Capt Bradbury who I'm sorry to say died soon.

He was awarded a Posthumous V.C.

J.A.

Above: In the vicinity of Signey Signet during the prelude to the Battle of the Marne, 8 September, 1914. A shrapnel shell has just burst behind the transport with the photographer himself (R.C. Money) hit by a spent ball. The despatch rider has been hit in the head as Money pressed the shutter release.   *R C Money*

Opposite above: 'You no shoot we no shoot.' The Christmas Truce, 1914.   *Walter Mockett*

Opposite below: 4.5 inch howitzer ready for action.   *K W Brewster*

Below: October, 1914, and SS *Franconia* brings home to Dover some of those who have escaped the unhappy consequences of the Antwerp expedition.   *J E Nicol*

My Dear Charlie,   28/12/14.

I am writing to let you know that I am still alive and well, we are in billets at present, we came out Boxing morning, so that we came spent part of Xmas out of the trenches. Xmas Day was spent by us in a most remarkable way, the Germans and our fellows got out of their trenches and shook hands with each other, the Germans said 'you no shoot, we no shoot', so we agreed, and all day long we walked about on top of the trenches, where in the ordinary course of events it would have been instant death for us. I went over and talked to some of them, they said they were fed up with the war and were reddy to go home, I have a coat button, a hat badge and some cigarettes from one of them, some of them come from London and so speak fairly good English, opposite to us they are Saxons, who are not so bad as the Prussians, the Kaiser presented his men with cigars Xmas Day. I had a bath yesterday, this is the second time I've had a bath over here, we go to laundries mostly, they turn the vats into a bath, we have nice hot water and at some places we have our dirty clothes exchanged for clean ones. We had proper Xmas weather, snow on the ground, and the water in the trenches frozen. Now I must close, as I have a few more letters to write, wishing to be remembered to all at home and hoping you are quite well,   I remain,
                                                Your sincere friend, Wally.

Opposite above: 18 Pounder field gun in action at
Morslede in 1915.   *N M Macleod*

Opposite below: Ypres in 1915 after heavy
bombardment.   *N M Macleod*

Right: 'Nice bloody Doctor wouldn't treat a wounded
man.' Medical Officer at work, the Battle of Neuve
Chapelle, March, 1915.   *E C Deane*

Below: Royal Fusiliers in Support Trenches near
Ploegsteert.   *K W Brewster*

> the parapet that we did not get out for a bit.
>
> The show began for me when I got the message Capt Morgan is hit & is bleeding badly. I ran along the trenches to him fearful of finding a shattered wreck. Doubling round traverses, jumping over pools of blood, severed limbs with no owners shattered corpses & groaning wounded.
>
> A Gurkha with his right hand handed me his left arm torn off above the elbow & wailed 'Sahib Sahib!' & as I ran on I heard a Jock say "Nice bloody Doctor wouldn't treat a wounded man." Morgan seemed shrunk & about half his usual size & was very blue 5 wounds mostly in the lung & probably our own shell. I had him taken off

Left: Trousers off looking for 'visitors' — an attempt at delousing.
Reginald Rapp

Opposite: Dressing Station during 2nd Battle of Ypres, April, 1915.
E M Lyons

Below: Officers and their servants 'in front line trenches near Ypres'.
Reginald Rapp

Right: 'The Kaiser and his band' as depicted by 7th Battalion King's Liverpool Regiment.
S C Marriott

Opposite above: Armentières 1915 and officers of 6th Battalion South Staffs study newly received Trench Orders rather than searching for the address of the legendary 'young lady'.
H L Graham

Opposite below: Fishing in Belgian becks offering as much likelihood of success as keeping such water courses from draining into trench systems.
K W Brewster

Below: A Flanders landscape, 1915.
K W Brewster

Left: The front line, 'Brickstacks', 1915.
S C Marriott

Opposite above: Identification with one's job.
S C Marriott

Opposite below: Givenchy September, 1915, and 7th King's Liverpool Regiment HQ is shelled.
S C Marriott

Below: Bivouac in woods, La Bassée Canal, 1915.
S C Marriott

Opposite above: HQ Mess, 7th Battalion King's Liverpool Regiment, Allouagne.
S C Marriott

Opposite below: This side of a dangerous corner and a Brigade Staff confers. *S C Marriott*

Right: 'The most ghastly scene it is possible to imagine.' Gas and confusion at Loos in September, 1915, and amidst it all great deeds as attested by Private A G Dutton, 1/20 London Regiment, who wrote of a Captain Williams who organized a team of bombers to consolidate a position gained. 'He was so calm and cool all through it all and has won everyone's praise and will I certainly think, get a DSO which he thoroughly deserves and which will be most popular amongst us men'.
Letter illustrated, G W Grossmith (1st Battalion Leicester Regiment)

Below: Loos in 1916: looking at the landscape of last year's battle. *E A P Hobday*

I looked for my landmarks in the German line, to guide me to the right spot, but the smoke was impenetrable ... Everybody scattered; I went on, chancing I knew the way. Orders were running and walking in the direction of the German trenches, looking like ghouls, owing to the effect of the smoke helmets. I was stifled in my helmet. Out of the little rectangular window of mica I looked for a way over the ditches and shell-holes. I passed men gassed, and saw Brown, dying, motioning with his hand the way forward. I shall never forget the sight till my dying day — the most ghastly scene it is possible to ~~imagine~~.

I crept blindly forward, a percussion bomb in one hand and holding my helmet tightly round my neck with the other. Then I came across some of my men lying in a row, waiting for the gas to clear before going forward. I joined them, and found the air more breathable; so took my helmet off, with unspeakable relief.

Here I consulted my compass, to try and find out the direction of their trenches, although I knew it would not tell us our lateral position. We went forward, and got to their wire, only to find it intact. Now, the artillery always blow the wire to pieces with high explosive shells before an attack, so I knew we were in

Above: On constant alert, elements of 1/5 Battalion York and Lancaster Regiment
holding the line at a particularly dangerous corner of the Ypres Salient, 1915.

Barnsley Chronicle Picture Library

Above: South African Subaltern, Hugh Saunders, soon to distinguish himself in the
RFC/RAF.   *H W L Saunders*

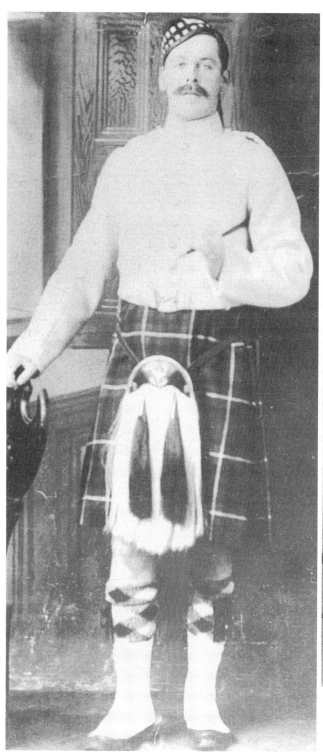

Above: Cpl Cyril Bassett VC, New Zealand
Engineers Divisional Signals.   *A E Alexander*
Left: Cuthbert A.S. Bean, Canadian Scottish
                                        C A S Bean

Above: Pte W.M. Clark, 10 Battalion Australian Imperial Force   *W M Clark*

Right: Subedar Mir Dast VC, 55 Coke's Rifles Frontier Force on his return from
France, Kohat, December, 1915.   *R G E Ekin*

Above: Machine-gunners of the 48 Pioneers in action at Shaiba, Mesopotamia, 12 April, 1915.
W E Spackman

Left: A soldier of the King's African Rifles
W W Newton

Opposite: Tom Clogstoun and his Nieuport in Palestine. *May Justice*

Below: West Indian Gunners who manned batteries defending Bridgetown, Barbados.
Matthew Richardson Collection

WIDER HORIZONS

**The War in the Air
The Dardanelles and Gallipoli
The Maritime Challenge
Soldiering in distant parts**

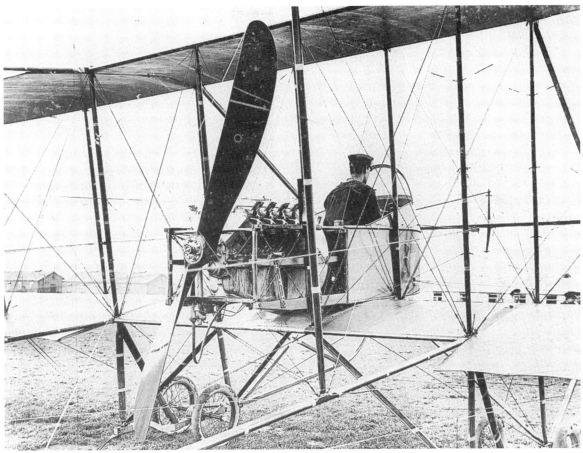

Above: 'If a bird can escape the rigging it's incorrect.' A Maurice
Farman Shorthorn being serviced.   *R E Nicoll*

Opposite above: German Naval Zeppelin L33, one of twelve raiding
England on 23 September, 1916, was damaged by anti-aircraft fire,
lost gas and was forced to land at Wigborough near Colchester.
In landing she caught fire; the crew was unharmed, being arrested
by policemen. Forty people were killed and 130 injured as a result
of bombs dropped on this raid. Two Zeppelins were lost.
                                          P Haig Ferguson

Opposite below: A family going to an air-raid shelter during a
daylight raid in 1917.   *(National Museum of Labour History, Manchester)*

Right: Air raid alarm! (Maroons were rockets fired to give warning
of a raid.)   *Mrs Phyllis Toms*

THE MAROONS

Left: RFC 'other ranks' framed by their tent.   *E Vousden*

Opposite above: Lieutenant P. Thompson pilots his Bristol Fighter over Essex on Home Defence duties.
G T Stoneham

Opposite below: 39 Squadron RFC (North Weald) on Home Defence duties, 1916.   *G T Stoneham*

Below: 56 Squadron RFC before going to France enjoy a concert at their Home Defence airfield, London Colney (1916).   *E Vousden*

Right: All wrapped up and somewhere to go: 2nd Lieutenant
Baldwin Raper, Hounslow, 1916 (19 Reserve Squadron RFC).
M M Kaiser

Opposite above: The airfield on Mafia Island during the aerial
search for SMS *Königsberg* in the Rufiji delta.   *C H Grenfell*

Opposite below: Seaplane reconnaissance, East Africa.
C H Grenfell

Below: Air mechanics Hutchinson and Robertson of the famous
60 Squadron.   *J W Rayner*

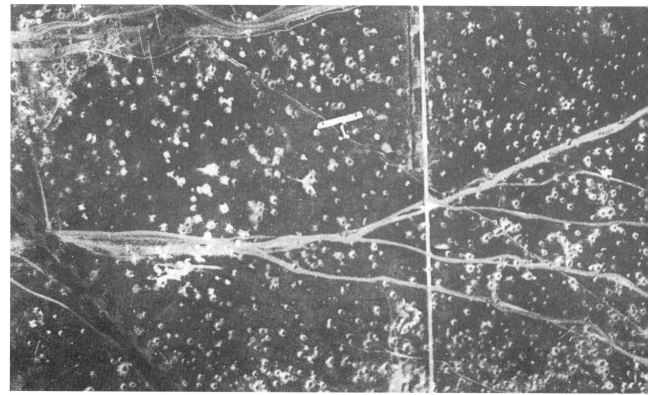

Right: Lieutenant H.W.L. Saunders RFC, Northolt 1917. *H W L Saunders*

Opposite above: Royal Naval Air Service Number One Wing (Dover Patrol). Christmas Greetings 1917.   *F G Horstmann*

Opposite below: A photograph of an enemy aircraft taken by W. D. Tisdall of No 8 Squadron RFC in June 1917.   *W D Tisdall*

Below: Royal Naval Air Service personnel examine a Sopwith Triplane.   *R E Nicoll*

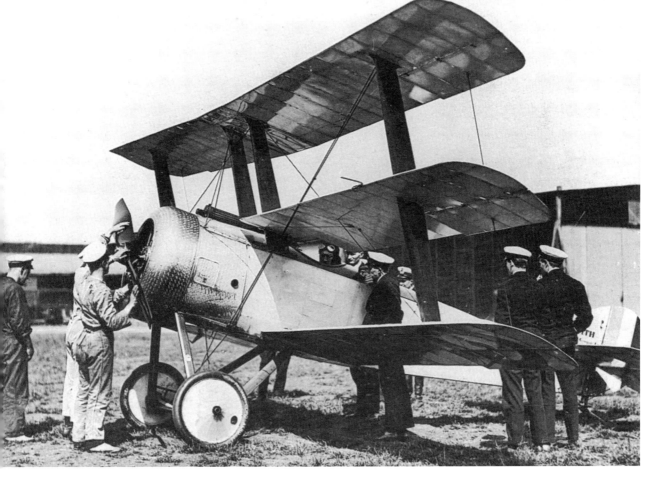

Right: Captain Rayner, a member of 60 Squadron's star football team.
J W Rayner

Opposite above: It looks as if there's something to celebrate. Note the monocles considerably in evidence and the hockey stick.   *J W Baker*

Opposite below: Waiting for the call. 66 Squadron RFC pilots at Vert Galand, France, May, 1917.   *O T Boyd*

Over the page: An SE 5a pilot of 60 Squadron. His last victory and another one 'unofficially out of control'.   *J W Rayner*

Below: Flying boat being towed to Heligoland Bight for a bombing raid.   *P Haig Ferguson*

44 b hr 45 mins

Date and Hour	Wind Direction and Velocity	Machine Type and No.	Passenger	Time	Height	Course	Remarks
24-10-18		S.E.5A. D6953	Self	2·15	12,000	O.P. No E.A. seen	
25-10-18		"	"	2·20	16,000	O.P. 7 Fokker seen E. of Quesnoy - climbed to get above but they went East when approached - attacked 5 Fokker over	
26-10-18		"	"	2·15	16,000	BERLIAMONT - Got 1 in flame - Maar + Burbridge 1 one each o/c (Also claim one unofficially out of control)	
						O.P. No Fokker seen - Back Harper got an L.V.G. which throttle	
						sub in out - Observer jumped in parachute to avoid disaster then	
27-10-18		"	"	2·5	2000	Visiting line saw L.V.G - did not attack	
14-11-18		F5587	"	1·45	5,000	Line patrol - none - Maubeuge - Avesnes - returning by night	
15-11-18		F5471	"	1·25		"	
		W "	"	1·45		"	
16-11-18		E4070	"	50	3000	Practice Wing formation	
19-11-18		D6007	"	15	10000	Engine test - O.K. (new engine)	
"		C8907	"	30	2000	Wing instruction - abandoned.	

Above: Sentinel over a trench siesta: Cape Helles, Gallipoli Peninsula (Lord Brassey's visit).   *Christine E Taylor*

Above: Lieutenant N. D. Holbrook (with arms folded) and the crew of the old
submarine B11 soon after the December, 1914, exploit of torpedoing the Turkish
battleship *Messudieh*.   *L S Ormsby Johnson*

Below: HMS *Lord Nelson* and the official diary for 18 March, 1915, when the
allied warships entered the Narrows of the Dardanelles to bombard the Turkish
forts at close range. The British lost two old battleships and, with greater loss of
life; the French lost their battleship *Bouvet*.   *James Friel*

```
18-3-15.    General attack on the narrows.
            Attack opened by "QUEEN ELIZABETH" "LORD NELSON" "AGAMEMNON"
            and "INFLEXIBLE" then older ships were sent closer in covered
            by fire of heavy squadron.
            2.45 p.m. "BOUVET" listed, and.sank. 4.10. p.m. "INFLEXIBLE"
            mined 4.13.p.m. "IRRESISTABLE" listed 6.0.p.m. "OCEAN" listed
            3.32.p.m. Mine sighted from fore top of "LORD NELSON" close
            under bow, went astern and avoided it, shortly after this 2
            mines were sighted, one on either beam, both were sunk by
            fire from Picket Boats.
            7.0. "CHELMER" came alongside with survivors and herself
            badly holed.
            Hits received:- Right gun of P.1 hit and split. Fore Top
                            hit, short distance W.T. shot away.
            Mr.Paul in Picket Boat picked up 7 survivors of "BOUVET" and
            also went alongside "IRRESISTABLE".
            Casualties :- P.O.Greenside wounded.
                            Expended:- 12" - 60 with full charges.
                                 9.2" -138  :    :      :
```

Above: Eve of the landing at Anzac: Australians head for the Naval rendezvous.
C F H Churchill

Right: 25 April, 1915, SS *River Clyde* about five minutes before beaching herself. 'Destroyers standing by for first sweep — transports coming up.'   *L A K Boswell*

Opposite above: The Australian and New Zealand landings taking place, 25 April, 1915.   *L A K Boswell*

Opposite below: A photograph taken on board SS *River Clyde* before she was run aground at V Beach, Cape Helles on 25 April to attempt to land the men cooped up in her holds.   *E H Tunnell*

Below: A photograph taken on SS *River Clyde* now run ashore at V beach, 25 April, 1915. Note, on the right, soldiers sheltering beneath the shingle bank covered from Turkish fire.   *E H Tunnell*

Above: General Birdwood leads Vice Admiral de Robeck and General Godley into the gap leading to the perilous No 3 Outpost, Anzac Sector, Gallipoli. An Australian soldier salutes but he must also see that the normal procedure is kept of a tally of those going through and those who return.   *L S Ormsby Johnson.*

Opposite above: Men of the Nelson Battalion, Royal Naval Division, on board HM Transport *Minnetonka* listening to their Officer in Command, Colonel Evelegh, explaining what was to be done elsewhere on the Gallipoli Peninsula while they acted out a dummy landing in the Gulf of Saros.   *J E Nicol*

Opposite below: Anzac shoreline with stores, landing jetty, a good deal of activity and some relaxation. *C F H Churchill*

Right: Royal Naval Air Service armoured cars impressively dug in but useless in or out of their Cape Helles 'garage'.*E H Tunnell*

Above: A less than high class shave for Lieutenant the Hon. Francis McLaren, MP, Royal Naval Air Service.   *F G Horstmann*

Opposite above: Holy Communion, Cape Helles, on the Gallipoli Peninsula (Lord Brassey's visit).   *Christine E Taylor*

Opposite below: Cooked breakfast with dusty seasoning.   *F G Horstmann*

Right: Royal Naval Air Service casualty, Lieutenant the Hon. Arthur Coke.   *F G Horstmann*

Above: Stores being unloaded from the Motor Lighter 'Beetles', Suvla Bay, August, 1915.
L S Ormsby Johnson

Left: Mail from home lures troops at Suvla Bay.   *G Speir*

Below: Lala Baba and the final gun position being prepared before the evacuation of Suvla Bay.
G Speir

Above: U boat and victim: (a captured German photograph).   *E L Berthon*

Above: The sailing ship *Medway* takes a sea on board.
C E Black

Opposite above: 24 January, 1915, and the Battle of Dogger Bank. HMS *Tiger* on left, SMS *Blücher* disabled and sinking, to right. *P Haig Ferguson*

Opposite below: 1915, The sailing ship *Medway* becalmed. *C E Black*

Right: A sailor's stunt at Malta, April, 1915. A rating reaches HMS *Trent* via the hawser linking her to the quay. *C H Grenfell*

Above: Port Said and it is very hot but the ship's company of HMS *Trent* still has its morning exercise.
C H Grenfell

Opposite above: A scourge scotched. SMS *Königsberg*, Rufiji delta, observed by officers of one of the monitors which had shelled her to destruction, HMS *Severn*.
C H Grenfell

Opposite below: Men of the King's African Rifles prepare to disembark from HMS *Severn* in the Tukuledi River, for a raiding party, German East Africa, June, 1917.
C H Grenfell

Left: King Neptune and his consort hold Court aboard HMS *Swiftsure*, crossing the line in March, 1916.
E T W Church

Right: U boat and victim, (a captured German photograph).   *E L Berthon*

Opposite above: Initiates pay tribute to King Neptune aboard HMS *Swiftsure*.   *E T W Church*

Opposite below: U boat victim (a captured German photograph).   *E L Berthon*

Below: What fate lies in store for the seated ship's boy and his shipmate victims? A captured German photograph.   *E L Berthon*

Above: Last sweep before the Battle of Jutland and a tragic fate.
HMS *Queen Mary* (*Princess Royal* and then *Lion* beyond *Queen Mary*).
P Haig Ferguson

Opposite: Jutland and its aftermath. The diary of Midshipman Woodhouse aboard
HMS *Lion*.
F C Woodhouse

Below: King George V visits Rosyth Naval Base 15 June, 1916, and speaks to the
officers and ratings of HMS *Lion* and the battlecruiser squadron of which *Lion*
was flagship.
Liddle Collection

MAY, 1916.　　　　　Week.　　　　　JUNE, 1916.

Sunday 28　(149-217)　Rogation Sunday.

Thunderstorm in afternoon, but it was quite warm. Party went away in whaler & landed below slept on deck.

and church as usual. Had afternoon watch. Fine afternoon. Left watch till 7. the bridge. Played Units in evening.

Monday 29　(150-216)　Rogation Day.

Coaled ship 5.40 a.m. - 4.20 a.m. Did high angle range finder handbook in forenoon. Read 13.5 drill in afternoon. Turret drill in B Turret in evening. Slept on the upper deck.

Thursday 1　(153-213)　Ascension Day.

Nothing in morning after all. Went round the damage in forenoon with Mr McCay. All dead men were aft. Wounded in Admiral's cabin so needed. Packed up Action at about 4 pm. Buried 89 men 6 officers at sea in evening. Steam watch whole goodbye. Blew fairly hard at night & sea got very rough. came down.

Slept [...] all that night in aft [...] the 4" in A turret.

Tuesday 30　(151-215)　Rogation Day.

Went away in cutter in morning. Control in forenoon. Went into Argo Tower. Played cricket at Grange Ground Edinburgh in afternoon. W R v G R. Molyneux & self played for W R because they had not got through. Grand 11. Raised steam in evening. 1st & 2nd BCS & 5th BS went out at about 11pm BST. Had middle watch.

Friday 2　(154-212)

night defence 9 submarine watch till 7.45. Arrived at 9.30 & were closely guarded by soldiers at the bridge. Coaled 1250 tons. Finished at 6 pm. Men absolutely dead tired. Got the wounded out before coaling. Started ammunitioning at 6.30 pm. A Turret taking in 99 cordite A P.

Wednesday 31　(152-214)　Rogation Day.

Lovely day. Divisions in forenoon. Got a war aft. Left submarine watch in forenoon. Did nothing in afternoon. Action sounded. Action sounded about 3.4.5. Opened fire at 4.37 on 5 German battle cruisers. Finished firing at 10.30. Remained closed up all night. Going to be in action again in morning.

Saturday 3　(155-211)

at 2.30 am. Finished ammunition at 2.30 am. Looked round for bits of shell & went down to armourless & to galley & aid lay & canteen. Went ashore with Butler to Edinburgh & Saw Auffles. so Jordan's. Had tea at the Navy Went ashore in the Crystal because all our boats were out of action. Turned in fairly early.

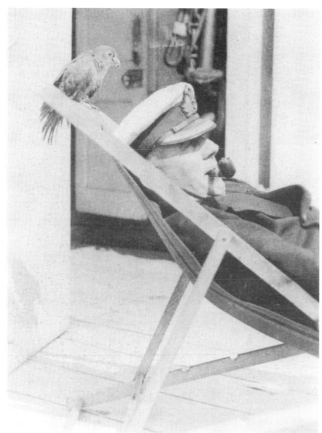

Left: Principal Medical Officer sitting pretty (HMS *Roxburgh*).   *J E Nicol*

Opposite above: Ratings examine the propellers of HMS *Lurcher* damaged after hitting an underwater obstruction.   *P. Haig Ferguson*

Opposite below: A German mine taken for examination aboard the Steam Yacht HMS *Sagitta*, Flagship of the Officer in Command of Mine Sweeping in the area.   *James Corry*

Below: Deck hockey, HMS *Roxburgh*.   *J E Nicol*

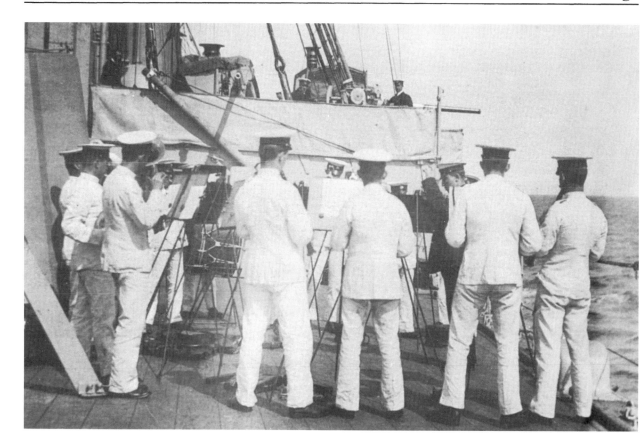

Above: Informal inspiration. The Bishop of London aboard HMS *Colossus. F Bowman*

Opposite above: Royal Marine Band, HMS *Roxburgh*   *J E Nicol*

Opposite below: Royal Naval view of Manhattan Island, New York in 1917,
Woolworth Building left centre.   *J E Nicol*

Below: An RNAS non-rigid airship, piloted by E. H. Bellew and with Midshipman
W. F. La R. Beverley aboard, in some distress in the North Sea.   *W F La R Beverley*

Above: Houton Bay in the Orkneys and a sack race for men of HMS *Colossus*.
F Bowman

Opposite: Armed and readied troopship making headway off Land's End. Note the lifeboats swung out and the fore and aft guns trained outboard.   *S W Lushington*

Below: Convoy off Land's End. *S W Lushington*

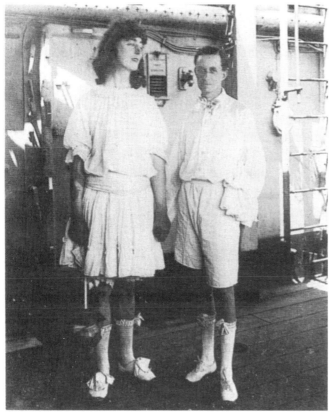

Left: Naval officers at play, Elvise (Lieutenant Mansfield RN) and Clarence (Surgeon Lieutenant Woods RN) entertain shipmates.   *G H Bickmore*

Opposite above: A successful U boat attack in the North Sea on destroyer Flotilla Leader HMS *Scott*, 15 August, 1918.   *P Haig Ferguson*

Opposite below: The Navy salves an aeroplane in the Heligoland Bight.   *A B Combe*

Below: Boxing aboard HMS *Tiger* in Rosyth.
P Haig Ferguson

[Handwritten manuscript, two columns]

Piers.

The harbours were alight with star shells; and several batteries opened out on us and began hitting.

We saw the Stroom Bank Buoy lit German fashion away to the North East altered up about 16 points for it and passed it on our stab bow. Her Co. S60°E

We realised to our dismay that the wind was blowing South th it absolutely the wrong direction and so there were Brilliant and Sirius with two ML's one on each quarter steaming in towards a whole array of searchlights and other lights. The entire horizon were flooded with light. Star shells were bursting above us and to seaward. Blue devils eight these shells tied together with wire came hurtling through the air making an infernal noise and heavy stuff hit us on the f'sle. One round hit the water on the Stab side of the Bridge and burst covered us with bits and with water, no one was hurt but we all had to spit a lot to get rid of the taste.

On and on we went, my duties were to con the ship and follow Brilliant and so I was fully occupied. The flaming onions were thriving

devil and really put the wind up me. Somehow or other as if gripped by some power which came from up above, I was quite myself. We were being hit hard and regularly and the machine guns were firing like blazes at us. The whole world was filled with light, one heavy shell hit us on the port quarter and stove in fins, another shell hit us Starboard side of the pole and a fire began in the Sick Bay. I knew precious little of what was going on as I had my hands and mind full with managing the ship and keeping close to Brilliant. We could not see any piers; the Huns had put up such a smoke barrage round them that nothing had no C.M.B or precious few could see them. We certainly could not see anything. The time limit on S60°E had been reached, we reduced to slow. Hell had been let loose, every machine gun every big gun was firing at us two. It was just like day between us and the coast and star shells burst continually above us. One shell took off the top tkind of the foremost funnel. One could feel it. Suddenly Brilliant and us closed. one each

Above: The Zeebrugge/Ostend Raid 23 April, 1918; HMS *Sirius* was used as a block ship for Ostend and an officer admits that fulfilling his responsibilities and 'some power which came from above' enabled him to be 'quite himself' even though 'every machine gun every big gun was firing at us'.

E L Berthon

Below: A sick or wounded soldier's painting in the autograph album of a VAD nurse.

Miss A Storey

Above: A concert party piano is loaded aboard river gunboat *F2* at Kifl to follow
the advance up the Euphrates in Mesopotamia in 1917.   *R C Morton*

No.1   Douglas McIntyre
from Newcastle to Boulogne c375 miles

McIntyre was an office boy in a Newcastle upon Tyne spice-importing firm. He enlisted in the 3rd Battalion Northern Cyclists in June 1915 and in April 1917 was transferred to the 6th Battalion King's Own Yorkshire Light Infantry. On 17 July 1917 Corporal McIntyre sailed for France and during his service was badly gassed.

No.2   Bill Mather
from Sheffield to Salonika c2411 miles

Mather was a University student engaged voluntarily in munitions work. He enlisted in February 1916. The regiment with which he served overseas was the 8th (Pioneer) Battalion, Oxford and Buckinghamshire Light Infantry. By ship he left Southampton on 1 February 1917 for Le Havre and a train to Marseilles. He left Marseilles by boat on 10 February and arrived at Salonika for service in Macedonia on the 16th of that month.

No.3   Charles Pearce
from Newlyn to Bombay c7074 miles

From Cornwall, a Territorial and a Regimental Quartermaster Sergeant of the 4th Battalion Duke of Cornwall's Light Infantry. He left Southampton aboard the troopship *Assaye* 4 October 1914, arriving at Bombay 9 November for service in India, then Aden, Egypt and Palestine.

No.4   Jack Nicol
from Greenock to Gallipoli c3859 miles

A coal merchant of Greenock, a Royal Navy Volunteer Reserve Officer, Greenock Division, served in the October 1914 Antwerp expedition and then in March 1915 went by troop transport to the Eastern Mediterranean for the Gallipoli campaign. Later in the war his service took on a more 'Naval' character in HMS *Roxburgh*, a cruiser on convoy duties in the North Atlantic.

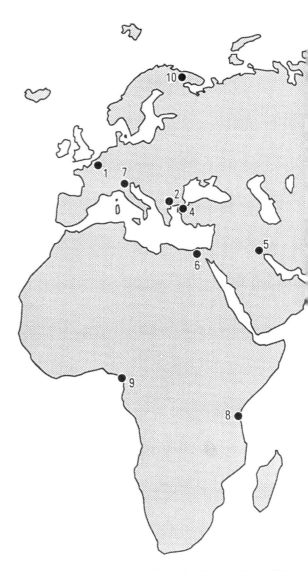

David Appleyard, School of Geography, University of Leeds. 1994

No.5   John Hammond
from Oswestry to Basra c4721 miles

Working as a postman Hammond volunteered in February 1916 and had little training before being sent overseas. On 21 May 1916, a sapper in the Royal Engineers, he left Devonport and, via the Suez Canal, reach Basra 14 June. He served the remainder of the war in Mesopotamia.

No.6   Harry Lowe
from Tarporley to Alexandria c3541 miles

A farm labourer and a private in the Ches Yeomanry, for which Regiment he volunteere October 1914. His regiment sailed for the M East 3 March 1916, aboard SS *Haverford*, arr in Alexandria 14 March. Harry transferred to Imperial Camel Corps and served in Egypt Palestine.

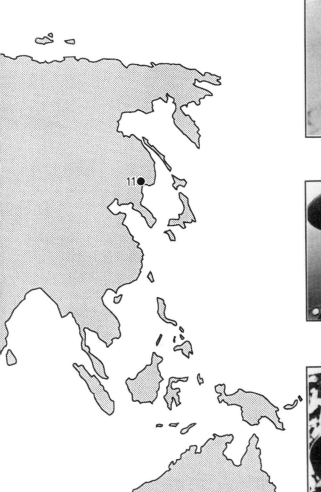

No.11 Walter Hartley
from Sudbury to Vladivostok 13,885 miles

Hartley was a private in the 9th Battalion Hampshire Regiment. On 3 February 1916 he sailed aboard HMT *Ceramic* for India, where he served until the end of October 1918. On 29 October 1918, his battalion sailed from Bombay via Colombo, Singapore and Hong Kong arriving at Vladivostok on 25 November 1918 for service in Siberia against the Bolsheviks.

No.10 Harold Blezard
from Burnley to Murmansk c1495 miles

A weaver of Burnley, Lancashire, Blezard joined the 8th Battalion East Lancashire Regiment and later transferred to the Machine Gun Corps. Aged 19 he served in France, was wounded and awarded the Military Medal. On 18 September, 1918, he embarked on SS *Loamadon* and sailed for Murmansk, North Russia, arriving there 27 September.

No.9 Dr Norman S Deane
from Rothkeale to Duala c6169 miles

Doctor Deane had only recently qualified in County Limerick, Ireland, when war broke out. He had been appointed to the West African Medical Service and on 18 August 1914 he left Liverpool in the SS *Elmina* for Freetown, arriving 28 August. In September he volunteered to serve as Medical Officer with the British West African Field Force campaigning in the Cameroons. There were further adventures for him after this successful campaign because, in January 1916, whilst aboard the SS *Appam* with some German prisoners, they were intercepted by the converted German merchantman *Moewe*. After some days of uncertainty *Appam*, minus some gold bullion it had been carrying and of course its German prisoners, was allowed to proceed to North America.

No.7 Digby Stone
from Streatham to Legnano c951 miles

A Londoner and a private in the 2nd Battalion Honourable Artillery Company he went to France before the end of 1916 and was there promoted to Lance Corporal. In November 1917 he entrained at Abbeville and travelled via Paris, Marseilles, Genoa and Legnano for service in Northern Italy in the final twelve months of the war.

No.8 Dr James Elmsly Mitchell
from Albrighton to Mombasa c9827 miles

Doctor Mitchell left his medical practice in Shropshire to take a commission in the Royal Army Medical Corps. On 5 April he sailed from Devonport bound for Durban in South Africa. His letter on landing records 'the novelty of the situation was immense'. His subsequent service was further north in the East Africa Campaign.

Left: More familiar with armoured car transportation, Petty Officer Ernest Tunnell tries the ship of the desert.
E H Tunnell

Opposite above: Civilities preserved, pyjamas and a shave, Sinai. *G Speirs*

Opposite below: A Ford car which failed to reach Baghdad in 1917. *C R S Pitman*

Below: The Second Battle of Gaza, 26 March, 1917, and men of the 4th Essex Regiment advance in extended order towards their objective (marked with a cross). 'Bert Peters lies here, I was wounded and notice the gaps where [our] boys have fallen.' *E Abrams*

Above: Temporarily at rest in Mesopotamian mud
– a bullock tonga RAMC cart.   *V H W Dowson*

Opposite above: Armoured car officers,
Mesopotamia.   *V H W Dowson*

Opposite below: Street entertainment,
Mesopotamia.   *V H W Dowson*

Left: The beggars of Baghdad; the unfamiliar
becomes familiar.   *V H W Dowson*

Above: India and the North-West Frontier; troops wait before moving into the Shurki Tangi Pass.   *F G Banks*

Opposite above: A new overseer – Briton in Baghdad.
V H W Dowson

Opposite below: Cameroons, 26 October, 1915; E Company, West African Rifles lands from the Senega River to march on Edea under Lieutenant Minniken. See the roof of the right-hand building; is that a framed net for catching birds?   *N S Deane*

Right: Ancient and Modern dispatch riders, India.
F G Banks

Above: A break in communications, Northern India. *F G Banks*

Opposite above: Not cricket coaching but bombing instruction for Indian Army recruits at Cannanpore June 1918, (83rd Wallahabad Light Infantry). *Ronald E Greenhouse*

Opposite centre and below: A British Officer (Pigot) takes Indian Army recruits for physical exercises after a morning 'dip'. The 83rd Wallahabad Light Infantry at Shamiapett, near Bolarum. September, 1915. *Ronald E Greenhouse*

Left: Imperial partnership – Gurkha and RAMC Ambulance driver. *V H W Dowson*

Left: King's African Rifles, No 1 Coy. British NCO's with two orderlies in the lines near Entebbe, East Africa.   *F O Stansfield*

Opposite: 'I will never laugh at a Ford car again'... 'Man eating lions growl round our camp at night'... Encounter with a local chief, his magic man and his other wives. Two letters from an Army Service Corps Officer describe the problems of campaigning in East Africa.   *N Whitehead*

Below: A Regimental Band leads the way; King's African Rifles on a route march.   *F O Stansfield*

16 June 16

My darling Daddy,

I have been too overworked to write for ages but my C.O. has given me two days off to rest in, so I am writing letters home.

I am keeping a daily diary ever since I left England so that you can read it when I get home again. It is the chance of several lifetimes to be under General Smuts; he conducts operations like greased lightening [sic]. The Infantry moving practically at the double and the transport being forcibly shoved day and night over mountain passes, through sandy desert land with thorn bushes, up to their axles in sand, through boggy wastes, and straight through jungle with men with axes making roads as they go. I used to grumble at the roads in Flanders; now we sigh for anything half so good — I have even taken convoys straight through bush velte [sic] crashing down the bushes as we went. My car and lorries have upset and run away backwards and forwards in the passes. If a lorry breaks its spring one chops down a tree and blocks it up with wood. Every lorry with four wheels and a running engine is shoved on somehow. We are on half rations, but the country teems with game and grouse, partridges etc — also with man-eating lions; these growl round our camp at night.

I will never laugh at a Ford car again, it is a miracle of engineering, it is not only far away the cheapest car on the market but it is easily the best and most capable car that there is for this sort of work, I have taken my Ford in places where no other car could have reached to save its life and if it is well driven and looked after it is a very sweet running car.

17 June 1916

The other day I halted my convoy for the night in the middle of the mountain pass at about 6 pm. It appears that I stopped near the residence of an important native chief. At about 6.30 he payed me an official visit — He was dressed in a toga formed from a bit of bright red flannel with several rusty nuts and bolts let into the lobe of either ear. Round his ankles and arms were wound old scraps of wire, and his face, arms and legs were pipe clayed white. His head was shaved with the exception of one tuft on the top, a la poodle.

In his hand he carried a ragged umbrella with the handle broken off.

He had a retinue of about eight following him carrying his bow and arrows and another with a spear, a third with a metal studded club etc, and last but far from least, his "magic man". He was stark naked with rows of beads and old bits of sardine tins etc strung all round him, his whole body was painted in various colours, his head was shaved. In his hand he carried a large knife.

The magic man terrified me; and during the whole interview he danced round us brandishing his knife and screeching like a madman.

I saw his show arriving from about a quarter of a mile and guessing what it might be I collected my dictionaries and a YMCA phrase book to start and end the interview. The native chief stopped in front of me and clapped his hands so I did ditto and then I sat down in my deck chair and he sat on the ground with his attendants standing.

He asked me how many wives I had with me and when I answered 'none' he said something to an attendant who darted back to the chief's residence. In about a quarter of an hour he came back with several girls who were all in a state of nature with the exception of one who was the chief's sister. All these were offered to me as a stop-gap and I had the greatest difficulty in getting the chief to take them away. The idea was that I could have the chief's sister and my men the rest. In return for this kindness I gave the chief a box of matches, a tin of bully beef, and one or two empty tins of petrol; he appeared delighted and went away — This was by far the swellest chief that I have yet seen.

Right: Frank Taylor, an official photographer with the Expeditionary Force in North Russia. *F Taylor*

Opposite above: The original caption of this photograph of transportation problems in Macedonia is 'send for the horses'. *R W Stenhouse*

Opposite below left: Making friends with the locals outside what Chief Petty Officer Horstmann called their 'Pub'. Lemnos, Eastern Mediterranean. *F G Horstmann*

Opposite below right: Changing the guard, 'Oxford Circus', Murmansk, North Russia. *F Taylor*

Below: The Seres Road, Macedonia, and a Gunner starts the day with a wash and a shave while one element of his unit's transport shows either patience or stubborness. *R W Stenhouse*

Above: A Christmas card for British troops in Italy shows
an appropriate setting in every sense.   *Liddle Collection*
Right: Macedonia, and a concert party rehearses.   *R W Stenhouse*

Below: A battery's transport on the move in Macedonia.
                                                     R W Stenhouse

THE HOME FRONT

Women and Children in Wartime
The Industrial Scene
Food Production, Economy and Rationing
Fund-Raising, Voluntary Endeavour and 'Life Continues'

Above: A schoolboy's curiosity, Stoneleigh, Reigate, 1916.   *G T Stoneham*

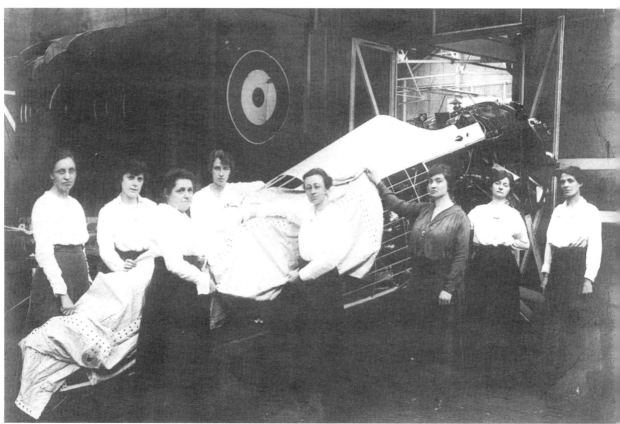

Women and Children in Wartime

Right: Women ready for action and victory. Munitions girls of Hornsby's of Grantham played their one and only football match against a men's team of fellow workers. Sportingly or complacently the men played with one hand tied behind their backs. They lost 1-0.
Malcolm Baxter Collection, Grantham

Opposite above: Heavy work in a brewery yard but a smile for the camera.
Bass Brewery Museum, Burton upon Trent (86.1196.01)

Opposite below: At Ruston Aircraft Production Works, Lincoln, women find a new use for fabric. From left to right, Miss Cooling, Miss Beresford, unknown, Miss N Masters, Miss E Brittain, Maggie, the Foreman Miss Barron and Miss Leverington.
Museum of Lincolnshire Life, Lincoln

Below: Women engine cleaners of Grantham, 1917, engaged specifically as substitute labour, initially at 5d an hour for a 44 hour week and with the use of a uniform. By 1918, in the summer, they were working for 24/- for a 50 hour week.
Museum of Lincolnshire Life, Lincoln (D1120)

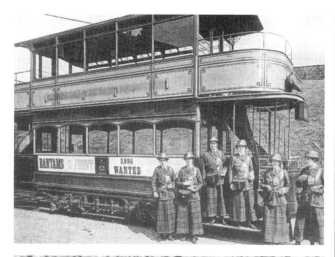

Above: Saying 'cheese' and with cheeses, Land Army girl 'Wills' at the dairy, Combe Lancy. *Mary Gibson*

Top left: Conductresses of the Glasgow Tramways. They are wearing a green tunic and Black Watch tartan skirts. Their service is necessary because of the exodus of men from the Corporation Tramways to fill the Glasgow Tramways Battalion of the Highland Light Infantry. *Glasgow District Libraries*

Left: Combe Lancy, Devon; 'Arbon and Dot at stable door'. *Mary Gibson*

Above and left: Vera Tregenza 1916 VAD nurse and at
school in 1914.　　　　　　　　*F E Gilpin*
Below: Farewell picnic for wounded about to be discharged,
Waverley Abbey, Auxiliary War Hospital, Farnham.
　　　　　　　　　　　　　　　May Justice

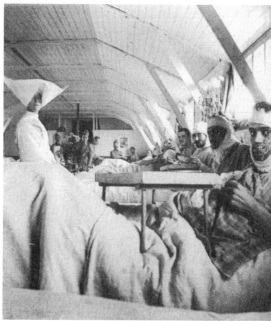

Right: This looks very much like surfboarding. It is labelled 'Miss
F Botha, Maud, Muizenberg'. Nurses off duty?   *Miss C Taylor*

Opposite above left: Waverley Abbey Auxiliary War Hospital
(Farnham). VAD nurses give a concert as 'The Squarettes' 25
July, 1917.   *May Justice*

Opposite above right: 'Cookee' learning to cope with steps at
Waverley Abbey. 'Larry' and nurse May Justice (on the right) at
hand to help.   *May Justice*

Opposite bottom left: Englishwoman May Corballis, as Sister of
Charity Sister Marguerite, in France in August, 1914, received the
permission of her Order to do Field Ambulance work at Roubaix
in the first days of the war. As the Germans occupied large sections
of North-Eastern France, Sister Marguerite, by persuasion and
strength of character, won from the Germans the right to continue
her medical ministrations. Furthermore, by argument and repeated
appeal (even to the German Emperor) she was allowed to return
to France in late 1916. She nursed in 1917 in the Verdun sector
and for her work she received both the Croix de Guerre with Palm
and the Legion of Honour.   *Sister Margueritte (May Corballis)*

Opposite bottom: With French wounded at Souilly, 1917.
    Sister Marguerite (May Corballis)

Below: Blanche Dunn, leaning against the windscreen, smiles
besides the friendly faces of her Women's Royal Air Force and
Royal Air Force colleagues at the Transport Depot, Salisbury.
    Mrs B Davies née Dunn

DRILL SERGEANT (low to the W.A.A.C). SQUAD, SHUN! NOW, LADIES, hold your heads up.— SHOULDERS WELL BACK AND The THUMB IN LINE WITH THE SEAM OF THE TR——— I MEAN —ER (RESPERATELY.) SQUAD STAND AT EASE!

Above: Words of command and male confusion.
Miss Hilda Greenhouse

Opposite: 'I am to go to the trenches ... every night at 6.45 will you pray for me and I will pray for you.' A soldier to his sweetheart.   *John Alfred Corkhill/Lettice Kneale*

Right: Women's Auxiliary Army Corps cooks at Caterham Barracks.   *Emily May Lane*

Below: Orcadians for whom life changed little unless in the immediate vicinity of Kirkwall and Scapa Flow.*F Bowman*

On Active Service

WITH THE BRITISH
EXPEDITIONARY FORCE

Address reply to

Name *Jack*

√ Section   √ Company *1st* Battalion *King's* Reg!

N° *3030?*

THE BRITISH EXPEDITIONARY FORCE,
c/o GENERAL POST OFFICE,
LONDON.

*Rouen
France*

*Monday
13th March* 1915

My Darling Leecie,

At last the news has come through and I am to go to the trenches to-morrow night. I do not feel timid and yet I dont like the idea, however I joined to fight so I am not grumbling.

In case I do not come through darling, I will have you in my thoughts to the last, you know that I love and live for you and now when I recall past memories both bright and dark, I think you are a perfect brick to stick to me like you have done. God bless you for it.

I dont like writing this sort of letter to anyone especially you dear, but I must show my feelings to you at this time.

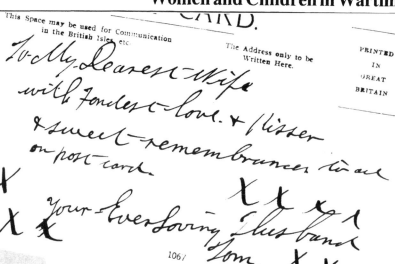

Thoughts from Witley Cam[p]

❖

* MEMORIES. *

How sacred are the memories
That linger in my mind,
Of happy times and blessed hours,

[G]OD BLESS MY DEAR SOLDIER BOY.

God have You in His keeping
Wherever You may roam,
God bless and shield You ever, dear,
And bring You safely home.

Will send washing tomorrow Love.
My Dear Loving Husband,
*   Received your letter this morning Wed not much news Love,*
however, don't be afraid I shall not forget you for it makes me
think of you knowing that you would like a baby. How do you like
the post card, don't you wish it was me in your arms — I do.
Don't feel funny Love and don't forget to get on to them don't leave
it a long time or you will never get. I am not neglecting you if it is
only a card Your my loving husband.
*   Your ever loving Wife Emily.*

Opposite: Hearts apart; Private Tom Meredith and his wife Emily attempt to bridge the gap with correspondence. Tom was to be killed.   *Tom and Emily Meredith*

This page: 'Carry this for luck old man'; bullet-torn last messages from the wife and daughter of Sidney Kaye, 1st Battalion King's Own Yorkshire Light Infantry, killed in action 24 May, 1915

"Think of me."

Think of me. Sweetheart![1]
    When the woods are gay
With buds of Spring, & thick with sheeted blue
Down all those ways I went last year with you
Think of me sometimes sweetheart —
      Think of me.
      2.

Think of me, River.
    When your long Tide
Washes the idle prows along the shore
Rattles the oar that I shall wield no more
Think of me, dear old River —
      Think of me.

Think of me, London.[3]
    When the sunlight streams
On Bond Street's jewelled windows all ablaze
Hyde Park, S. James', dim in golden haze —
O many - memoried London
      Think of me!

Think of me, England![4]
    Though my grave be green
Far from thy shores, and War a dream long past
It was for thee they laid me here at last —
England — I loved and died for —
      Think of me!

              Margery Lawrence
              1918.

Above: Margery Lawrence, bereaved, writes poetry as if composed by her fiancé,
A. L. Stewart, killed in action 21 March, 1918.   *A L Stewart*

Opposite: Photograph and souvenir serviette from the wedding of Gertrude May
Cohen of Brixton and Second Lieutenant David Stross of Leeds, Brixton Synagogue
14 September, 1915. David Stross was to lose his life in flying training. *Audrey M Godfrey*

SOUVENIR

In Commemoration of the

Marriage between

Second Lieutenant David Stross,

fifth son of Mrs. & the late Mr. S. Stross of 6, Harehills-Avenue,
Chapeltown, Leeds.

AND

Gertrude May Cohen,

eldest daughter of Mr. & Mrs. J. Cohen of 14, Grove-road, Brixton.

At the Brixton Synagogue, Effra-road, on Tuesday Sept. 14, 1915.

All Blessings and Happiness to the

> Darling Mother & All, If ever you receive this letter, I shall have passed away from this world.
>
> Please don't worry, I have only died as so many others have died, for my Country's cause. I honestly believe we are fighting in a righteous cause. Our deaths are steps to victory.
>
> Please accept my most sincere thanks for all you have done for me during my life. I only regret to say that I have not lived longer to show my appreciation. I owe everything that I have been or done to you.
>
> Please don't mourn my death unnecessarily, I have only passed to another world where troubles & pains are unknown.
>
> God give you all strength to live long & happy lives. Goodbye. We shall meet again
>
> Yours with all my love Walter.

Above: The most unwanted letter of all, delivered in the event of the soldier's death. 'Please don't worry, I have only died as so many have died, for my country's cause.' Second Lieutenant H. W. Goodson, killed in action during the last year of the war.

H W Goodson

Above: Evelyn Greig, aged eighteen months, and referred to in wartime family letters as 'our little sweetheart', and one can see why.   *Dorothy Greig*

Above: Two children at Holcot, Northampton, dressed for a church fête as a wounded soldier and a Red Cross Nurse.
Mrs Y Snell

Above: Children outside the walls of Cardiff Castle play their part in encouraging the 'doing of one's bit', 1914.   *Glamorgan Archive Service*

Below: A domestic science class at Canning Place School, Glasgow, 1916/17. Note the ink wells in the desks in the foreground, the cooking range, utensil racks and the dress of the girls.   *Strathkelvin District Libraries*

Above: Children's war games, Cathcart, Glasgow, 1915.
By courtesy of the Herald and Evening Times, *Glasgow*

Below: Tynehead School, Garrigill, Cumberland, in early 1917.
Beamish, North of England Open Air Museum

for twenty mile route marches. Some of you lads will go for those when you have holidays. You will find them most enjoyable

Many of you girls would laugh to see your poor old teacher scrubbing floors and washing up. You probably could teach me a few useful lessons. I am sure I need them. On Thursday last, I was Cookhouse fatigue and my duties included, the scrubbing of tables and cupboards. and the cleaning out of pans. There was grease up above my elbows. Hurry up lads! Learn now how to sew on your buttons and, darn your socks. or you will probably change your views one day as to who lead the more useful lives. boys or girls.

I miss you all very much and my greatest regret is, that I shall probably not have the pleasure of again teaching some of you. By the time the war is over several of you will have left school. I should like to feel assured that you are making the most of your opportunities and supporting your teachers in every way. Do all you can to fit yourselves for the life that lies before you and you can best do it by learning. diligence, strict attention to duty and by setting out always with a high purpose. Above all value your honour beyond everything else.

With all good wishes,
I remain.
Your sincere friend
F. W. Lamb.

Above: A schoolmaster, F. W. Lamb, now a soldier in training, writes to his former pupils of Auckland School, County Durham. Every child in his class wrote him a letter each month and he replied in a letter to them all.

Doris Roberts (at the time in Mr Lamb's class)

Above: James Neilly and his son, William, of Jellyhill, miners at Cadder Colliery,
Bishopbriggs, just north of Glasgow, 1915. *Strathkelvin District Libraries*

Right: Miner Dick Stokoe hewing coal at West Wylam Yard Seam, just North of the River Tyne.
Beamish, The North of England Open Air Museum (19874)

Opposite above: A Merchantman entering No 6 dock Cammell Laird and Company, Birkenhead, for repair or refit, 6 May, 1915.
Cammell Laird Archive: Wirral County Council

Opposite below: The 'shell scandal' of 1915 being tackled.   *National Museum of Labour History, Manchester*

Below: Girls who kept the boys going; munition girls at Thorpe, Wakefield, wearing their uniform and badge, the latter represented in the design held by the girl in the front row.   *Mrs B Cushion*

Above: Workmen at Messrs Richard Hornsby and Sons Ltd of Grantham, Lincolnshire, where shells were filled for the Admiralty.   *Museum of Lincolnshire Life*

Opposite: Girls at work, Barnbow Munitions Factory, Leeds.   *Leeds City Library*

Below: Derby Locomotive Works now manufacturing munitions; women making fuses in No 10A shop.   *Derby Industrial Museum*

Above: Workers and product at William Foster and Company Limited, Lincoln, production birthplace of the Tank.   *Museum of Lincolnshire Life, Lincoln (D1605)*

Opposite: Barnbow Munitions Factory, Leeds, after the explosion of 18 May, 1918, in which James Thompson of Harrogate, William Orange of Leeds and James McHale of Leeds were killed. In a previous explosion at this factory in December, 1916, thirty-five had been killed, and in March of the following year there were two further fatalities as the result of an explosion.   *Leeds City Libraries*

Below: Cardiff women assembling aircraft frames in 1918 in the converted White, Wilson's mattress factory at the northern end of Penarth and Ely Harbour Road.   Cardiff Yesterday *(No 16:50)*

Above: The scale of a problem. Cammell Lairds excavated a new basin to build
and float out this huge Admiralty dock.   *Cammell Laird Archive: Wirral County Council*

Below: Cammell Laird Shipyard; The destroyer USS *McDougal* in dry dock for
repair in 1918.   *Cammell Laird Archive: Wirral County Council*

Above: With U boats sinking vessels close inshore the taking of these fish exposed
fishermen to more than just bad weather. *Beamish: The North of England Open Air Museum*

Above: A family snap in the poultry run, Muirside, Glasgow.
Glasgow District Libraries; (Baillieston Collection B1/17)

Opposite above: Little Miss Beveridge and her grandmother outside their shop and home in Baillieston, Glasgow in 1916.   *Glasgow District Libraries*

Opposite below: Public schoolboys till their land, Truro College.   *F E Gilpin*

Below: Women's Land Army girls and soldiers assist in baling with a Fowler steam engine at Leverton near Boston, Lincolnshire.   *Museum of Lincolnshire Life, Lincoln*

Above: Teesdale sheep shearing.   *Beamish, The North of England Open Air Museum (14441)*

Below: Herring gutters at work on Scotland's northern coast in the summer of
1918 when Wick was still the largest herring port in Europe. *St Andrew's University Library*

Yorkshire Agricultural Society

in conjunction with

The University of Leeds and
The Yorkshire Council for Agricultural Education

have arranged a

DEMONSTRATION

OF

Motor Ploughs and
Tillage Implements

to be held by kind permission of THE FARM COMMITTEE, at

The North Riding Asylum Farm,
RAWCLIFFE,

Two Miles from York Station,

THURSDAY & FRIDAY, Nov. 4th & 5th, 1915,

Commencing at 10 a.m. each day.

Light Refreshments will be provided on the Ground by
Messrs. T. E. Cuthbert & Co., Ebor Hall, York.

Taxis or Cabs may be engaged at York Station.

Further particulars can be obtained from *John Maughan.*

Secretary, Yorkshire Agricultural Society,
BLAKE STREET, YORK.

Above: Mechanization and modernization of farming equipment. The same
authorities who arranged this demonstration were also to encourage the use of
sulphate of ammonia in the manuring of crops for the spring of 1916.

Leeds University Archive

(2593.)   Wt. P1099/2066.   1,000,000.   6/17.   P.P.Ltd.   Est. 1386.   F.C.—4.

Mr. Slice o'Bread.

"I am a Slice of Bread.

I measure three inches by two-and-a-half, and my thickness is half-an-inch.

My weight is exactly an ounce.

I am wasted once a day by 48,000,000 people of Britain.

I am 'the bit left over'; the slice eaten absent-mindedly when really I wasn't needed; I am the waste crust.

If you collected me and my companions for a whole week you would find that we amounted to 9,380 tons of good bread— **WASTED!**

Two Shiploads of Good Bread!

Almost as much—striking an average— as twenty German Submarines could sink— even if they had good luck.

When you throw me away or waste me you are adding twenty submarines to the German Navy."

National War Savings Committee, Salisbury Square, E.C. 4.

Left: Save us this day your daily bread.
Malcolm Baxter Collection, Grantham

Opposite: Avoiding the waste of the fat of the land.
Malcolm Baxter Collection, Grantham

Below: The harvest of barley sown on Mitchell and Butlers Brewery recreation ground at Cape Hill, Birmingham. At the Bass Museum there is a bottle of beer brewed from this grain.
Bass Brewery Museum, Burton upon Trent (86.0026.00)

F.S.B. 11.

How to

eke out

JUNE, 1918.

the fat

L ARGE quantities of fat are required for the manufacture of explosives. If every housewife or cook who is visited by a rag and bone merchant would take the trouble to save and sell to him the grease from washing-up water, the total amount of fat thus collected, instead of choking the drains, would be of great service to the country.

The fat collected from Army camps has produced—

(1) Tallow sufficient to provide soap for the entire needs of the Army, Navy and Government Departments, with a surplus for public use.

(2) 1,800 tons of glycerine for ammunition—sufficient to provide the propellant for 18,000,000 shells.

To be obtained from—

MINISTRY OF FOOD,

DESPATCH DEPARTMENT,

35, PARK STREET, W.1.

2606. Wt.   /   12 pfs. 50,000(2). 5/18. S.O.,F.Rd.

Above: 'The Lincolnshire Hoemanry'. Men employed to hoe potatoes on a Sunday at the Gride, Old Leake near Boston in 1917. They were paid £1 a day.   *Museum of Lincolnshire Life, Lincoln (D1179)*

Opposite: Powerful posters encourage household economy.
    Malcolm Baxter Collection, Grantham

Left: Price control on butter beans.   *Malcolm Baxter Collection, Grantham*

Below: Ministry of Food National Ration Book.   *Mary Gibson*

NOTICE

BEANS, PEAS AND PULSE
(RETAIL PRICES) ORDER, 1917

The Food Controller is advised that Japanese Diafuku Butter Beans should be classed as "Butter Beans" and retailed at the price fixed for "Large Butter Beans."

G. WALTER ROFFEY,
for the Secretary.

N75 W1.16058/280 96.000 7/17 J.P. Gp 138

13 SPARE	7 SPARE	1 SPARE
14 SPARE	8 SPARE	2 SPARE
20	9 SPARE	3 SPARE
	10 SPARE	4

Right: Harvest work on a Devon Farm, Combe Lancy, Devon 1917.   *Mary Gibson*

Opposite above: Roath, South Wales: housewives queue for rations from the Home and Colonial Store at the corner of Albany Road and Inverness Street.   *Mary Gibson*

Opposite below: 'Fidgets' parades in the ring, Combe Lancy, Devon.

Cardiff Yesterday *Series (16 no 192)*

Below: German prisoners of war seem to be doing the heavier work on this farm, Combe Lancy.   *Mary Gibson*

I hope M: Bob is keeping well it is a very trying time for everybody our two boys were well when we heard last- I do wonder how Miss Winnie is now- I hope she is not suffering very much.

I expect the food rationing does not affect you yourself very much as you are. such a small eater I'm nearly always hungry

we did not get a scrap of (week before) Cheese last) and last week 6 ozs we miss cheese more than anything for Fred to take to work with him one day all he had to take for his dinner was 2 apples & bread it would not be so bad if he could come home to dinner I've got plenty potatoes & had a nice lot of greens.

J.G.H. Gao

BY THE KING.

A PROCLAMATION.

GEORGE R.I.

WE, being persuaded that the abstention from all unnecessary consumption of grain will furnish the surest and most effectual means of defeating the devices of Our enemies and thereby of bringing the war to a speedy and successful termination, and out of Our resolve to leave nothing undone which can contribute to these ends or to the welfare of Our people in these times of grave stress and anxiety, have thought fit, by and with the advice of Our Privy Council, to issue this Our Royal Proclamation, most earnestly exhorting and charging all those of Our loving subjects the men and women of Our realm who have the means of procuring articles of food other than wheaten corn, as they tender their own immediate interests, and feel for the wants of others, especially to practise the greatest economy and frugality in the use of every species of grain: And We do for this purpose more particularly exhort and charge all heads of households to reduce the consumption of bread in their respective families by at least one-fourth of the quantity consumed in ordinary times; to abstain from the use of flour in pastry, and, moreover, carefully to restrict or wherever possible to abandon the use thereof in all other articles than bread: And We do also, in like manner, exhort and charge all persons who keep horses to abandon the practice of feeding the same on oats or other grain, unless they shall have received from Our Food Controller a licence to feed horses on oats or other grain to be given only in cases where it is necessary to do so with a view to maintain the breed of horses in the national interest: And We do hereby further charge and enjoin all Ministers of Religion in their respective churches and chapels within Our United Kingdom of Great Britain and Ireland to read, or cause to be read, this Our Proclamation on the Lord's Day, for four successive weeks after the issue thereof.

Given at Our Court at Buckingham Palace, this Second day of May, in the year of our Lord one thousand nine hundred and seventeen, and in the Seventh year of Our Reign.

GOD SAVE THE KING.

Above: A Royal Proclamation to 'practise the greatest economy and frugality in the use of every species of grain'.
Reverend H F Westlake

Opposite above: Yvonne Snell watches her aunt cut the first sods in a Golders Green, North London, allotment. In Yorkshire, the University of Leeds and the Yorkshire Council for Agricultural Education were stressing that allotments should be close to the 'allottees' dwelling houses or time is wasted in walking to and from the land and the journey becomes, in the end, irksome and irritating'.
Mrs Y Brown née Snell

Opposite below: 'I'm nearly always hungry.' Coping with the restriction of rationing.
J G H Gardner

Above: A poster makes clear that housewives have their own battlefront − the
shop and the kitchen.   *Malcolm Baxter Collection, Grantham*

Above: Jennie Jackson of Burnley, seen here with HM Queen Alexandra at Marlborough House in June, 1916, had raised £1,000 between February and June of that year to buy the fully equipped Motor Ambulance in front of which she stands. *Miss J Jackson*

Above and opposite: The Dug-out; a YMCA canteen in Bristol.   *I D Joss*

Left: Fund-raising stamps; a teenager's collection.   *Miss G Milburn*

BELGIAN REFUGEES IN LENZIE.

Above: Belgian refugees in Lenzie, Strathkelvin, near Glasgow. In the flight from Belgium as that country faced German occupation in 1914, many parts of Britain took the exiles. Here they pose seeming to find little about which to smile. The refugees were at first welcomed warmly, given assistance with housing and employment. In Lenzie they received free medical treatment. It should not be regarded as surprising that there were problems ahead for both refugees and hosts. Enthusiasm and gratitude were to wane, cultural differences appeared more obvious and for the hosts other preoccupations drew on their reservoir of sympathy and anxiety. *Strathkelvin District Libraries*

Opposite above: Soldier patients of Bishop's Knoll Hospital, Bristol, photographed with the Lord Mayor of Bristol at the zoo. The war pensioners in the centre include men who had seen service in the Crimean War. *I D Joss*

Opposite below: HM King George V and Queen Mary visit Beckett's Park War Hospital, Leeds. *Violet de T Towers*

Right: One wounded soldier here seems assured of company. *Violet de T Towers*

York Tank Week.

Bank at the Tank in the Market Place and help to

BUY MORE AIRSHIPS.

Britain's word is **HER** Bond and that Bond will win the War. Get **YOURS** now!

Dropped from a

British Airship.

Printed by the Yorkshire Herald Company, York.

Left: Fund-raising via the tank in the Market Place at York and the airship which dropped this card.
Liddle Collection

Opposite: A famous stand by the 51st Division in March, 1918, inspires a new song.   *L J Smith*

Below: With delightful originality the British Red Cross had inaugurated a goodwill 'Happy Thought Day'. Here in Grantham (July, 1916) Happy Thought Day, even if with a stern face, is in action as civilians with sidecars prepare to take wounded from Grantham's Red Cross Hospital for a day out in Stamford.
Malcolm Baxter Collection, Grantham

Above: War fails to stop play. Wham Cricket
Club seems to have kept its soldier son or
attracted one.
Beamish: The North of England Open Air Museum
(29469)

Opposite: Time deals cruelly with an image
such as this, undeniably reflective of the
wartime anxiety of mothers and children.
Liddle Collection

Right: Sunderland Ashbrooke Hockey Team
defends its goal.
Beamish: The North of England Open Air Museum
(35673)

Above: Foreigners attempt to protect themselves from anti-German harassment.
The National Museum of Labour History, Manchester

Opposite above: Leeds Town Hall and a hundred female University students classify the new National Registration forms in 1915, a step on the road to conscription – but not of women in this war.   *Leeds University Archive*

Opposite below: The Patriotic Pageant, a stimulus and focus for the imagination of West Country author, Minna Gray. She draws upon the past to stir up morale for the crisis dominating the present.   *Miss M Gray*

Left: Professor J. B. Cohen from the department of Organic Chemistry, University of Leeds, uniformed as a Special Constable in Leeds. His duty was as a lookout in the crow's nest of Leeds Town Hall and he shared his responsibilities with Professor A. J. Grant of the History Department.
Leeds University Archive

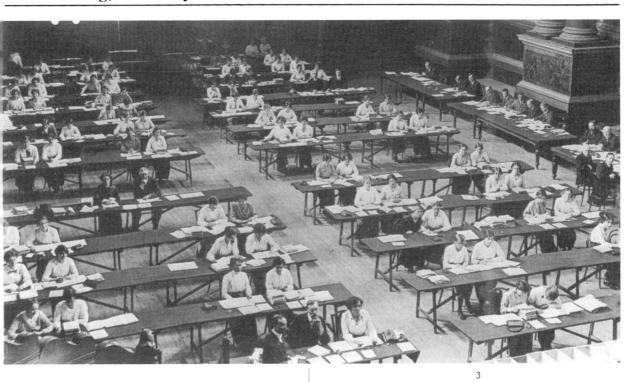

3

THE EMPIRE CALLS.

✤

Patriotic Pageant

FOR THIS YEAR OF WAR, 1915.

WRITTEN BY MINNA GRAY.

FOR ADULTS OR CHILDREN.

Suitable for representation either in or out of doors.

The Costumes can be arranged for a few shillings.

CHARACTERS.

EMPIRE—Imperial Crown, Sceptre and Orb, Purple Mantle and Ermine.

S. GEORGE—Silver Armour, Red Cross Shield, Sword.

BRITANNIA—Helmet, Shield, Trident.

ENVOY OF THE TOWN.

ROYAL HERALD—Royal Standard, Tabard, Trumpet with Flag.

CAPTAIN OF THE GUARD—Khaki.

SENTINEL—Khaki.

UNION JACK SINGERS (any number)—Scarves, Emblems and Flags.

COLONIES (any number)—Scouts, with Flags or Scarves with Names.

DOMINIONS—Scarlet Mantle, Helmet, Drawn Sword.

FRANCE, RUSSIA, BELGIUM, ITALY—See Cartoons.

FOUR HERALDS OF THE ALLIES—Tabards and Trumpets.

JIM, JOE.—Artisan's Dress.

WOUNDED SOLDIER.

DRUM AND BUGLES.

Pages, Courtiers, Maids of Honour, Scouts, Girl Guides, any Local Bodies, such as Ambulance Corps, Fire Brigade, etc., as desired.

Time—From 1 hour, according to Songs or Displays introduced.

PARISH ENTERTAINMENT DURING WAR-TIME.

In this year of grave national crisis, difficulty must frequently arise as to how to replace the customary festivities for Parish, School or Guild by something more suitable for the moment. With this object, a Patriotic Pageant is here given, capable of almost unlimited variation, to include almost any number of children or adults, and to make use of any such displays, drills or songs as may be available. Local Ambulance Corps, Fire Brigades, Nurses, Scouts or Girl Guides may all take part. If out of doors the Procession might be extended and developed, though it is quite effective in a fair-sized Hall.

The Pageant might be followed by tea, and sports for young and old, the value of the prizes being expended on comforts for the wounded, which can afterwards be given in person by the winners, at the Local Red Cross Hospitals. In the case of children, this is a specially happy arrangement, profitable and pleasant for the little ones, and much appreciated by the patients. Some might even go, on the first suitable occasion, to give them in costume, and so vary the monotony of convalescence.

Prizes will be liberally subscribed for if it is known they will ultimately find their way to the Hospitals ; and a goodly sum may be gained for War Charities from the sale of tickets or from gate money !

It might not be unsuitable to conclude the afternoon with Evensong and Intercession.

Such a Programme might be found very suitable for the general public on Bank Holiday, or for a single school or guild in any fair-sized room. The Pageant may be performed without fee or royalty, but a donation or small percentage of the profits might be paid to the writer—Miss Gray, Verese, Torquay—for the benefit of the Devonshire Regiment, to whom details should be sent in the event of a descriptive speech by the " Envoy " being desired, or any further information required.

Above: Lord Brassey's famous yacht *Sunbeam*, newly fitted out as an auxiliary hospital ship, here seen at Gibraltar en route for the Dardanelles in 1915.   *Christine E Taylor*

Left: Seventy-nine year old Lord Brassey at the wheel of *Sunbeam* heading for the Gallipoli Peninsula.
Christine E Taylor

Above: A conscientious objector, C. H. Norman, is handed over by the police to
army authorities outside court.   *A Rose*

Above: In February, 1915, an increase in rents sparked off a protest in Glasgow, particularly in the districts of Govan and Patrick. With so many men away from home, the protests were led by women. The government was forced to take action when the engineering and munitions workers threatened supporting strike action. The Rent Restriction Act was passed by Parliament forcing the landlords to back down.

By courtesy of The Herald and Evening Times, *Glasgow*

Left: A pacifist addresses men at an anti-conscription meeting. Glasgow Green, 1916.

By courtesy of The Herald and Evening Times, *Glasgow*

57 Gordon Sq. W.C.1.   31.5.17

Dear Comrade

Thank you for your letter of 23 May. I am sorry I couldn't acknowledge it sooner, owing partly to the meeting of the Nat. Com. entailing a lot of work, partly to having to go to Salisbury Plain to see Clifford Allen. The explanation you give of the resolution is just what I wished to know —

Hunter, of the Nat. Com., has been very busy with devising means of carrying out our resolution as to the work under the Home Office, & Ammon also — Just at the moment the Leeds Conference absorbs a certain amount of energy, but in a direction likely to be useful to all sections of the pacifist movement — Yours fraternally

Bertrand Russell.

Above: In June, 1917, over 1,000 delegates from labour organizations and peace movements attended a conference in Leeds to discuss means of ending the war. The philosopher, mathematician and anti-war campaigner, Bertrand Russell, writes here to Howard Marten, a Quaker conscientious objector just before the conference which Russell, Philip Snowden and Ramsay MacDonald all attended. There was talk of the establishment of soviets, but little support for the delegates when they returned to their trade union electors.

H C Marten

Above: A watercolour in the bound single-copy issue of a Friends Ambulance Unit magazine, *Carrefour* No 1.   *K H Green*

Opposite: A Seventh Day Adventist's court martial statement explaining his refusal to parade on the seventh day of the week. *J Howard*

Left: Many opposed to the war were able, within their conscience, to work in war zones for the alleviation of the suffering caused by war. Accordingly, they enlisted in the Society of Friends motorized and train ambulance units. These units attracted men who, from numerous religious, political and moral standpoints, were opposed to the war. This photograph is of Friends Ambulance Train No 16.   *A H Simpson*

"My Court Martial Statement."

Sir,

As a Christian and a believer in the Holy Law of God — The Ten Commandments — I observe as sacred the seventh day of the week, from sunset on Friday until sunset on Saturday, in accordance with the Fourth Commandment. (Exod. 20-8-11.

This period of time is consecrated by God, and should be used only to do His service, nothing should be done on that day which would displease Him.

For thirteen months I have been given the privilege of obeying my God in this matter, and have been given exemption from all parrades on that day, for which I am greatly indebted by those in authority. I am willing as I told my superior officers before, to do all in my power, and come as far as I possibly can with them, but if it is a case of separating me from my God or obeying them I must refuse the later, and accept the consequences.

During the last thirteen months I have willingly done Sunday-work, to make up the hours I have had free on the (Sabbath) Saturday.

This therefore is my reason for disobeying the order to parrade at Red Barracks, Weymouth, on the seventh day of September 1918.

I could not conscienciously do so, and as it is then a question of either obeying God or Man, I cannot under any circumstances allow myself to displease Him even if while obeying Him in what He has taught me I disobey the Commands of my fellow-men.

Signed:—
4350. J. Howard (Private)
5th Southern Company. R.C.E.
Salisbury Plain.

Bulford Camp.

Above: Tower Hill, London, March, 1916, and a protest meeting by 'attested married men' on the issue of Military Service Act and Conscription.

National Museum of Labour History, Manchester (P532B)

Opposite above: Anti-war identification membership card for the No-Conscription Fellowship.

H C Marten

NO-CONSCRIPTION FELLOWSHIP

A Fellowship for common counsel and action composed of men of enlistment age who are not prepared to take up arms in case of Conscription, whatever the penalties for refusing.

MEMBERSHIP CARD

To Mr. *Howard L. C. Marten*

Address *Cruber-How*
West End Av. Pinner.

Dear Comrade,

In response to your application we are glad to welcome you to membership of the N.C.F. We enclose the name and address of your ~~Branch~~ Divisional Secretary with whom you should communicate at once, and who will put you in touch with other members in your district

Yours fraternally,

Home Counties ~~Branch~~ Division

A. FENNER BROCKWAY, *Hon. Secretary.*
AYLMER ROSE, *Organising Secretary.*

Secretary *Mrs. F. C. Hann*

8 MERTON HOUSE
SALISBURY COURT, E.C.

4 Holmdale Mansions, Holmdale Rd W Hampstead.
N. W.

Left: Conscientious objector Norman Gaudie records in his diary that he has been forcibly drafted into the Non-Combatants Corps and sent to France. Once there he refused to obey orders and was court martialled – his diary records the sentence, 'Sat June 24 [1916] Sentenced to be shot. Commuted to 10 years penal servitude'.

Norman Gaudie

Right: A photograph of the Quaker, Howard Cruttenden Marten, the first conscientious objector at a military parade to listen to the pronouncement of his death sentence. The sentence was commuted to ten year's penal servitude. Marten, later from prison in England, accepted the Home Office Work Scheme by which he laboured in non-war work at a quarry. On the reverse side he wrote: 'Thy affectionate nephew Howard arrayed in the full regalia of his present office Quarryman of Dyce, Aberdeen'.

H C Marten

Below: Fifteen of the first seventeen conscientious objectors sent to France in 1916. Howard Cruttenden Marten is in the second row, second from the right. The men are photographed in Dyce Quarry, Aberdeen, where they are on the Home Office Work Scheme subsequent to their experience in France.

H C Marten

H. M. Prison W. Scrubs

30 - 3 - 1917.

Dear wife

    I am now in this Prison, and am in usual *health.*

If I behave well, I shall be allowed to write another letter about 7 weeks time *and to receive a reply, but no reply is allowed to this.* my sentence is 2 years

      Signature— Fred Banks

      Register No. 3496

Above: Fred Banks, a conscientious objector in Wormwood Scrubs, will be allowed to write a letter in seven weeks.   *Fred Banks*

TELEPHONE
FINCHLEY 227.

39, WOODSTOCK ROAD,
GOLDERS GREEN, N. W.

Oct.24th.1916

Dear Sir:-

I have received with much appreciation the
very generous letter signed by you and your comrades,
in which you very kindly refer to my services to the
men who have been making this great fight for liberty
of conscience. It is little that one has been able to
do by comparison with what one would have liked to do,
but it is a satisfaction to know that one's efforts have
not been quite in vain.

It has been a great pleasure in a sense to
have had the opportunity of doing something for the
barve men who have made such a noble stand for liberty
and right, and I am sure we shall all look back upon
this fight with satisfaction, feeling that we have done
something to make us more worthy of the enjoyment of
liberty.

With all good wishes to you all

I remain

Mr.H.C.Marten.   Yours sincerely

Philip Snowden

Above: Philip Snowden, an anti-war senior Labour Party politician, replies to a
letter thanking him for his Parliamentary support of conscientious objectors.

H C Marten

Bye the way dosent it make you feel sick when a man is allowed to get up in the House of Commons and threaten labour revolution if Compulsion comes in. He ought to have been shot where he stood. It wont be very long before the colonies begin to ask themselves the question 'Is England worth fighting for? New zeland has turned out the whole of her male populatio and has had thousands of casualties. What they can think of it I dont know

CHURCH OF SCOTLAND YOUNG MENS GUILD

King For & Country

WE SEEK THE KINGDOM OF GOD & HIS RIGHTEOUSNESS

Above: Aylmer Rose (on the right) leaving Clerkenwell Police Court of Remand
after the failure of his appeal against conscription.   *A Rose*

Opposite: A soldier's attitude towards those speaking against conscription.   *F Denham*

Opposite below: Artist Percy Horton, a socialist conscientious objector, who would
accept no compromise in his anti-war stance, has to accept the use of this unsuitable
notepaper for illustrations of fellow prisoners.   *Percy Horton*

Above: Armley Prison, Leeds, 'home' for many conscientious objectors.   *F Banks*

Opposite above: The Independent Labour Party, Dartmoor Prison Branch, meets with visitors (note the lady top right) for a photograph outside the prison, 1 September, 1917.   *H H Haynes*

Opposite below: Dartmoor Prison illustrated in Howard Marten's autograph album.
                                                                     H C Marten

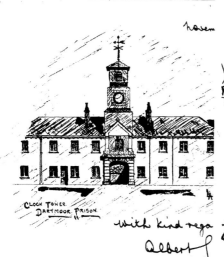

CLOCK TOWER
DARTMOOR PRISON.

We see in vision fair a time
When evil shall have passed away.

We live in strange & stirring times
And by the Law, when are we right?
FOR men of Peace, arrests & fines
The same as though we caused a fight.

Dartmoor, 1917

To the Army we are handed
And asked to do a little drill;
Then in the Guard Room we're banded
Because we say we will not kill.

Full of Hope, to us the future
(Though persecution our Faith tries)
But through the prison's aperture
The World's emancipation lies.

With kind rega
Albert L

Edwin A Arnold.

Muswell Hill. London. N.

Halifax Barracks.
Leeds Prison
Wormwood Scrubs
Leeds Prison
Escall Sawmills
Dartmoor.

Bradford.

Right: An armoured vehicle all quiet on the Irish Front during the Easter Rebellion in Dublin, April, 1916.
Peggy Goodwin

Opposite above: The ruins of the General Post Office, Dublin. Snapshot taken by Peggy Goodwin.
Peggy Goodwin

Opposite below: Liberty Hall, Dublin after the rebellion.
Peggy Goodwin

Below: Haddington Road, Dublin and the Easter Rebellion.
Peggy Goodwin

WAR DIARY

or

~~INTELLIGENCE SUMMARY.~~

(Erase heading not required.)

Army Form C. 2118.

Instructions regarding War Diaries and Intelligence Summaries are contained in F.S. Regs., Part II and the Staff Manual respectively. Title pages will be prepared in manuscript.

Hour, Date, Place	Summary of Events and Information	Remarks and references to Appendices
24.00. 29/4/16. DUBLIN.	Sniping by Rebels of Sinn Feiners Association continued throughout the day. Houses were searched for rebel arms and ammunition. The rebellion has by now developed into a system of home to/s warfare and Street Sniping. A large force of rebels is reported to be in occupation of BOLANDS BAKERY in LOWER GRAND CANAL ST. There have been no casualties in the battalion today.	
30/4/16. DUBLIN.	Only occasional shots by rebel snipers during the morning. Many suspected houses were searched but nothing of a suspicious nature arrived at BALLSBRIDGE. No heat is... Transport waggons arrived at BALLSBRIDGE. The French of the men is good only being under... rations have yet been issued.	
4.00 do.	117 rebels under Commandant de Alvera surrendered. They were disarmed and handed over to O.C. B Coy (CAPT. E.J. HITZEN). 6 A.P.M. at BALLSBRIDGE. searched and handed over to BOLANDS BAKERY, LOWER GRAND & CANAL ST. Their headquarters in BOLANDS BAKERY, LOWER R & CANAL ST. were searched and about 25 rifles of various makes (GERMAN, FRENCH) also sporting guns and rifles. Some 3000 rounds of ammunition were also removed. Much of this was of GERMAN origin in boxes labelled "SCHARFE PATRONEN". Many bullets were soft nose (soft flat nose).	

(73989) W4141—463. 400,000. 9/14. H.&J.,Ltd. Forms/Q.2118/10.

J.C. .... Colonel,
Comdg. 2/5th Bn. Lincolnshire Regt

Above: '117 rebels…disarmed'…Much of their ammunition 'was of German origin'. The war diary of 2/5 Battalion Lincolnshire Regiment, 29 and 30 April, 1916.
J C Urquhart

THE TEST WITHSTOOD

Civilian Internment
Serviceman Captivity
Western Front — the Somme to the End
The Armistice and Beyond

In November, 1914, the four and a half thousand British males caught in Germany at the outbreak of war were all gathered together and interned at Ruhleben Trotting Course on the outskirts of Berlin. So varied were the occupations of the internees that the community was able to provide fully for its social, educational, sporting, cultural and economic needs. The range of activity is indicated by the following photographs and documentation.

G and H Darnell

№ 1.   **Sunday, June 6th**   **1915.**

Absender: *E. R. Vincent*

Engländerlager Ruhleben

Baracke *XI* .

Box *14* .

March 17th 1915.

An To M *Dr Vincent* Ort *Hatch End*

"The Coppice", Middlesex -Straße No. ———

Write in pencil only. Nur mit Bleistift schreiben!

Dearest Father + mother.

Have just received Fathers P.C. of the 2nd + hope the cake he has sent will arrive safely. Since last writing have also received your letter of the 7th + box of cigarettes which I enjoy exceedingly. So very, ~~~~ sorry to hear in your card that my dog has been bad, (~~food~~, too much or exercise insufficient, I expect). For goodness sake dont let the children give him bread, + food scraps as Im sure he gets enough as it is. I must say that your letters + P.Cs come very well

Above: A student of Renaissance Italy replies to his first coded message from his parents. Deciphering was through the first word before a piece of punctuation and E. R. Vincent, the student, was here describing conditions in the camp and laying out the needs of the men interned. By coincidence this young scholar was to serve in cryptography in the Bletchley Park decoding establishment in the Second World War.

E R Vincent

Opposite: Except for those who had been to Boarding School or who had had any similar experience in communal living, an essential adjustment which all internees had to make was to the complete absence of privacy. Six men kept all their personal belongings and slept in what had been accommodation for a couple of horses.

A Salaman

Above: The blazered man wearing headgear must surely be the referee in this football match. League and cup competitions were held in several sports.   *H E Röhl*

Opposite above: The celebrated Ruhleben fire attracts a crowd, the City Fire Brigade and some volunteers.   *R B Croad*

Opposite below: A German airship passing over the camp — an impressive but not the most cheering sight to the inmates. Note the golfers to the fore!   *H E Röhl*

Below: A championship tennis match in play. Freddie Lane, a well known jockey, serves to J.C.Masterman, the supreme athlete and games player in Ruhleben, later to earn Secret Service laurels.   *H E Röhl*

Shakespeare Week.
"The Merry Wives of Windsor"
Mühleben 1917.

Left: Not apparently 'The Three Musketeers' but from 'The Merry Wives of Windsor', performed in the Shakespeare Tercentenary Week (1917).   *J Burgoyne*

Opposite above: Douglas Jones paints two internees and it is to be wondered how they got on with the merchant seamen, the professional sports coaches or the team of interior decorators held together in the camp.   *D D Jones*

Opposite below: The Casino, where you could dine in style even if somewhat frugally. Intriguingly, this photograph of waiters and a chef includes German guards, seldom pictured in other groups of internees.   *A Salaman*

Below: The orchestra and cast of Gilbert and Sullivan's 'The Mikado' pose in front of a grandstand.   *H R Lorenz*

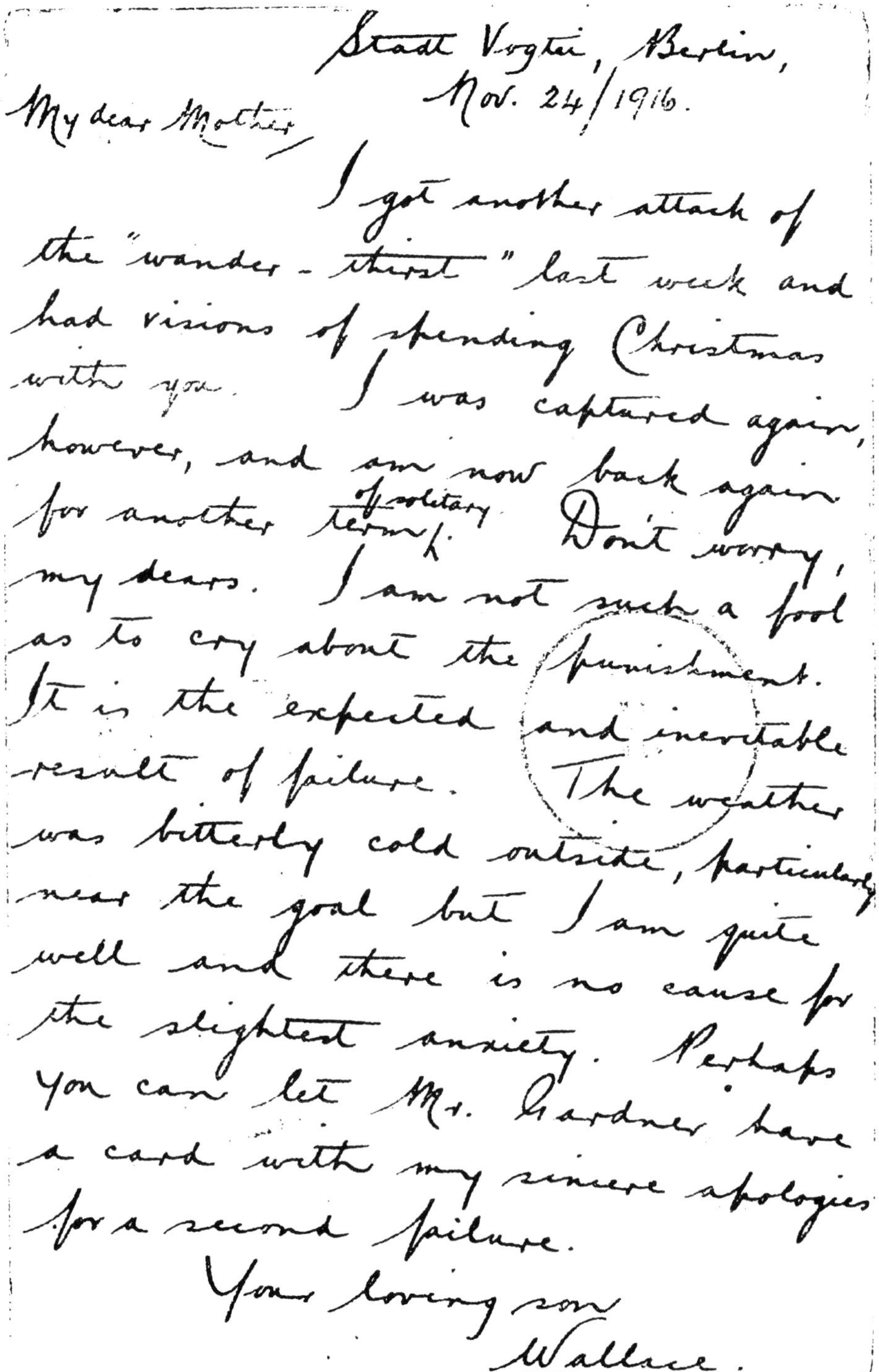

Stadt Vogtei, Berlin,
Nov. 24/1916.

My dear Mother,

I got another attack of the "wander - thirst" last week and had visions of spending Christmas with you. I was captured again, however, and am now back again for another term of solitary. Don't worry, my dears. I am not such a fool as to cry about the punishment. It is the expected and inevitable result of failure. The weather was bitterly cold outside, particularly near the goal but I am quite well and there is no cause for the slightest anxiety. Perhaps you can let Mr. Gardner have a card with my sincere apologies for a second failure.

Your loving son
Wallace.

Above: A letter home sent by Wallace Ellison after his second escape attempt.

W Ellison

Right: Wallace Ellison escaped from Ruhleben in July, 1915, and got within ten minutes of the Dutch border before recapture. He then served 113 days in solitary confinement in the Berlin City Prison (Stadt Vogtei). A second escape attempt in the following year also failed narrowly. His third escape attempt, in October, 1917, was successful. He was disguised as a German businessman and strode confidently past five sentries looking fully into the eyes of each one. He sepent four weeks and three days at large in Germany and planned carefully his crossing of the border into Holland disguised as a Krupps munitions worker. Back in England he lectured about his escapes and wrote books about them. He also worked for the British Secret Service in Switzerland. This photograph of Wallace Ellison was taken in November, 1917, when he was on the run, and was used on forged papers which helped him to cross into Holland.

PIER PAVILION

COLWYN BAY.

FRIDAY EVENING. FEB. 15TH, 1918

A PUBLIC LECTURE

Will be given by MR.

WALLACE ELLISON

ENTITLED:

"MY ESCAPE FROM GERMANY."

Mr. Wallace Ellison, after three attempts to escape from Ruhleben Camp and from Stadt Vogtei Prison in Berlin and several futile attempts, succeeded in getting away from Ruhleben on October 13th, 1917, and crossed the Dutch Frontier during the night of November 13th, 1917.

He spent the intervening four weeks and three days at large in Berlin and other German Towns.

Come and hear his thrilling narrative and his account of conditions in GERMANY AT THE PRESENT TIME.

The Lecture will commence at 7.30 p.m. prompt.

Reserved & Numbered Seats, 2/6; Balcony, 1'-; Back of Hall, 6d.
INCLUDING GOVERNMENT TAX

Seats may be booked at Messrs. Fleet & Son's Music Warehouse Penrhyn Road Colwyn Bay

"For nearly two hours he held an audience of 2,000 people enthralled." Southport Guardian, 11/1/18

Tomkinson Printer. Colwyn Bay. Tel. 195.

Above: Something about which to crow — outwitting the Hun and how it was done.
W Ellison

Opposite: Some notifications of the fate of British servicemen, missing and perhaps captured by Germans or Bulgars or Turks. *Liddle Collection*

This Form must accompany any Inquiry respecting this Telegram.

POST OFFICE TELEGRAPHS.

Delivery and Charges.

LESLIE SMITH & Co., Lond.

C. OR B.

Means ....
Distance ....
Collected ....
Paid out ....

If the Receiver of an Inland Telegram doubts its accuracy, he may have it repeated on payment of half the amount originally paid for its transmission, any fraction of 1d. less than ½d. being reckoned as ½d.; and if it be found that there was any inaccuracy, the amount paid for repetition will be refunded. Special conditions are applicable to the repetition of Foreign Telegrams.

Sent, or Sent-out

At ....
To ....
By ....

No. of Telegram

Office Stamp
MANCHESTER

Prefix Handed in at Office of Origin and Service Instructions Words Received here at

F 296 5HO OHMS KINGSWAY 52 =

THOMAS CARR 9 CARLTON TERRACE BLACKPOOL =

REGRET TO INFORM YOU THAT CAPTAIN T E A CARR R A
REPORTED MISSING TWENTYFIRST MARCH AAA THIS DOES
NECESSARILY MEAN HE IS KILLED OR WOUNDED AAA FUR
WILL BE SENT IF RECEIVED = MILITARY SECRETARY
INN FIELDS WC 2 :

Received at From By

B or C 3.

Кореспонденция на военно-плѣнни
(Correspondence of Prisoners of War).

БЪЛГАРИЯ

ПОЩЕНСКА КАРТА

COMITÉ INTERNATIONAL GENÈVE

AGENCE INTERNATIONALE DES PRISONNIERS DE GUERRE

Mrs. Frazier
29 School Road Moseley
Birmingham
England

P.W. 271

99001.

Br. F. S. Hudson
86 (Heavy) Battery
R.G.A.
(Presumably prisoner at Kut)

1) (Име) (Name)
2) (Народность) (Nationality)
3) (Чинъ) (Rank)
4) (Частьта отъ която е) (Regiment)
5) (Д-ъ се намира) (Dépôt)

R.I.P.

In Loving Memory of

Our Dearly Beloved Son,

L.-Cpl. Peter Alexander Dewar,

D Coy., 6th Batt. Gordon Highlanders,

Who was Wounded on 11th April

and taken prisoner,

Died at Verden-Aller on 26th May, 1918,

Aged 18 Years and 7 Months.

———

"He died that we might live."

Ashville.
Aberfeldy.

Above: Death in captivity. *Papers of J Hain*

Opposite: Fellow officer prisoners drawn by M. M. Kaiser, R.F.C. *M M Kaiser*

Left: 'I have one bit of bad news.' A wounded and captured officer writes with his left hand to break the news to his mother of the amputation of his right arm.

J B Longmuir

THE BRITISH PRISONER OF WAR

The Monthly Journal of the Central Prisoners of War
Committee of the British Red Cross and Order of St. John.

Vol. I.—No. 8   AUGUST, 1918   [Per annum. direct. including postage.]   Price Fourpence

Heidelberg. Summer 1915.   "Occupations of the idle rich."

Above and right: A naval officer records the open and the undercover activities of his fellow prisoners.

H H McWilliam

Opposite: The journal of the welfare organization for prisoners of war. Note that 'parchment-coated suet puddings' could be sent to them.   A N Barlow

Lagerbefehle.

1. Jeder Kriegsgefangene hat sich mit den Befehlen des Kommandanten vertraut machen, welche auf der schwarzen Tafel auf dem Flur der Kasernen und Baracken der Nähe des Eingangs angeschlagen sind, oder beim Appell bekannt gegeben werde

2. Die Kriegsgefangenen aller Nationen stehen unter den deutschen Kriegsgesetzen (§ Abs. 4 M.St.G.)

3. Die Befehle des Kommandanten und der deutschen Offiziere, sowie die Anordnunge der Feldwebel oder Unteroffiziere innerhalb ihrer Reviere und Befugnisse sind z befolgen, ebenso die Anordnungen der Posten und Wachtleute. Letztere habe Instruktion, ihre Waffen ohne Zögern in Fällen von Fluchtversuchen oder Ungeho sam zu gebrauchen.

4. Alle Kriegsgefangenen haben die deutschen Offiziere zu grüßen.

5. Es ist Kriegsgefangenen streng verboten Waffen, wie Säbel, große Messer, Revolve usw. oder Zivilkleidung zu tragen oder im Besitz zu haben. Es ist nur erlaubt Unifor und Uniformmützen zu tragen.

6. Jeder Offizier und Mann hat bei den Appells anwesend zu sein, die täglich 9 Uh morgens, und abends je nach der Jahreszeit zwischen 4 und 10 Uhr nachmittags a den dafür bestimmten Plätzen, das ist auf dem großen Dänholm vor Kaserne 6 un auf dem kleinen Dänholm zwischen dem Speisesaal und Baracke F abgehalten werde Befreiung vom Appell nur auf besondere Erlaubnis des Kommandanten.

7. Um 8 Uhr morgens muß jeder Kriegsgefangene, mit Ausnahme der Kranken, auf gestanden sein. Diejenigen, die sich krank fühlen, haben dies morgens dem Kasernen vorsteher zu [illegible] oder melden zu lassen.

8. Die Mahlzeiten sind in den Speisesälen einzunehmen, [illegible] kranke Offiziere können mit besonderer Erlaubnis des Kommandanten die Mahlzeiten auf die Zimmer gebracht bekommen. Frühstück von 7.30 bis 8.30 morgens; Mittagessen von 11.30 bis 1.30 nachm.; Abendessen von 5.30 bis 7 Uhr nachmittags.

9. Schlafenszeit ist von 10 Uhr abends. Von dieser Zeit an haben sich alle Kriegs gefangenen auf ihren Zimmern aufzuhalten. Das Besuchen anderer Zimmer nac 10 Uhr abends ist nicht gestattet. Es ist streng verboten in den Betten zu rauchen noch ist es erlaubt (Stearin)-Kerzen in den Zimmern zu brennen. Während der Nach hat Ruhe zu herrschen

10. Die Kriegsgefangenen können monatlich 2 Briefe und 4 Postkarten, oder im ganzen 6 Postkarten monatlich schreiben. Korrespondenz irgendwelcher Art von Kriegs gefangener mit der deutschen Bevölkerung und/oder mit feindlichen Ausländern, in Deutschland lebend, ebenso wie alle Korrespondenz mit Kriegsgefangenen in anderen Lägern in Deutschland, Oesterreich-Ungarn, der Türkei, Bulgarien usw. ist streng verboten. Alle Korrespondenz ist den Postprüfern durch Vermittlung der Kasernen vorsteher zu übergeben. Die ausgehende Post ist den Kasernenvorstehern am 1., 10., 20., eines jeden Monats abzugeben, an anderen Tagen werden keine Briefe oder Postkarten angenommen. Briefe und Postkarten sind in gewöhnlicher Sprache und und deutlich zu schreiben. Schriftstücke, die Codewörter, Chiffre, Stenographie oder Abkürzungen enthalten, werden vernichtet.

11. Der Inhalt der ankommenden Pakete wird auf der Lagerpost im Beisein des Empfängers durchsucht und gegen Quittung ausgehändigt. Verbotene Gegenstände werden konfisziert. Die Umhüllungen der Pakete werden nicht ausgeliefert. Blechdosen werden zurück gehalten und nur deren Inhalt wird ausgeliefert.

12. Gesuche an die deutschen Behörden sind in deutscher Sprache abzufassen. (Ausnahmen sind gestattet wenn sich kein Offizier im Lager befindet, der deutsch schreiben oder sprechen kann.)

13. Jeder Kriegsgefangene hat das Recht den Kommandanten persönlich zu sprechen und seine speziellen Wünsche, Klagen usw. vorzubringen. Sprechstunden beim Kommandanten täglich, mit Ausnahme des Sonntags, von 11.30 bis 12.30 nachmittags. Diejenigen die hiervon Gebrauch machen wollen, haben sich um 11.30 Uhr vorm. auf dem Flur vor der Kommandantur zu versammeln.

14. Besucher für Kriegsgefangene werden auf keinen Fall zugelassen.

15. Der Kommandant ernennt einen Lagerältesten für das Lager, sowie für jedes Zimmer einen Zimmerältesten. Im allgemeinen wird dies der dienstälteste Offizier sein. Die Aeltesten sind dem Kommandanten gegenüber für das gute Verhalten der anderen Offiziere verantwortlich, welche ihren Befehlen und Anordnungen zu gehorchen haben.

16. Die Namen der Bewohner jedes Zimmers sind auf einem Zettel an der Außenseite jeder Tür anzubringen und zwar numeriert, der Stubenälteste und sein Vertreter zuerst.

17. Jeder Offizier ist persönlich verantwortlich für die Ordnung und Reinlichkeit in seinem Zimmer sowie für alle Sachen, die ihm zum Gebrauch gegeben sind, wie Bett, Garderobenhalter, Schrank, Stuhl usw. Die Zimmer werden von den Burschen gereinigt und Türen und Fenster sind während der Reinigung offen zu halten. Während der Nacht müssen sämtliche Fenster geschlossen sein, nur die oberen Fensterklappen können offen bleiben. Offene Fenster sind einzuhaken.

18. Jeder Kriegsgefangene wird zur Verantwortung gezogen für irgend welchen Schaden, den er absichtlich oder durch mangelnde Sorgfalt macht. Das Zuschlagen der Tür ist verboten.

19. Es ist verboten irgendwelche Sachen, wie Möbel usw., die geliefert werden, anders als für den Zweck, für den sie bestimmt sind und dienen, zu gebrauchen. Teller, Pfannen, Kaffeekannen, Tassen, Löffel, Gabeln, Tischmesser usw., die durch die deutsche Behörde zum Gebrauch in den Speisesälen, Küchen usw. geliefert werden, dürfen nicht auf die Zimmer genommen und dort gebraucht werden.

20. Vorsicht beim Gebrauch der Kochherde, Oefen und besonders der Regulieröfen.

21. Liebesgaben, Eßwaren, welche den Gefangenen gesandt oder in den Kantinen verkauft werden, können auf den kleinen Kochherden, die für die Kriegsgefangenen besonders angeschafft sind und in den Kasernen und Baracken stehen, aber nicht in den deutschen Lagerküchen gekocht werden.

22. Das Angeln in dem Bassin zwischen dem Großen und Kleinen Dänholm ist nur vom Ufer des Kl. Dänholm aus erlaubt. Es ist strengstens verboten, im Park, auf den Wegen, Straßen, Feldern, in den Gärten und auf den Rasenplätzen nach Würmern zu graben. Ebenso ist es verboten Zweige, Laub, Blüten und Aeste von den Bäumen und Büschen oder Holz von den Gittern, Lauben und Bänken abzureißen oder die Gegenstände durch Schneiden zu beschädigen.

23. Es ist verboten die Rasenplätze zu betreten oder sich darauf zu lagern. Dies ist nur auf dem Grase zwischen der Hauptlagerstraße und dem Hafenbassin erlaubt.

24. Das Baden und Schwimmen in dem Hafenbassin zwischen Gr. u. Kl. Dänholm ist verboten.

25. Es ist streng verboten innerhalb des Lagers Fußball, Hockey oder Golf zu spielen.

26. Das Ausspucken auf die Fußböden der Kasernen und Baracken ist verboten. Es sind in den Räumen Spucknäpfe aufgestellt, welche auch dazu da sind Tabakasche, Zigarren-, Zigarettenstummel und Streichhölzer aufzunehmen. Es ist ferner verboten durch die Fenster zu spucken oder Gegenstände durch dieselben hinauszuwerfen.

27. Der Aelteste eines jeden Zimmers hat darauf zu achten, daß die Lagervorschriften von seinen Kameraden und den Burschen befolgt werden. Er ist verantwortlich für die Ordnung und Sauberkeit in seinem Zimmer und hat für Schäden aufzukommen. Ungehorsam seiner Kameraden oder der Burschen gegenüber seinen Anordnungen oder gegen die Lagerordnung hat er dem Lageroffizier zu melden. Nachdem der Zimmerälteste die Stube übernommen hat, ist er verantwortlich für die darin befindlichen Gegenstände.

28. Alles Privateigentum ist an den dafür bestimmten Plätzen aufzubewahren. Es ist verboten Nägel in die Wände oder Türen zu schlagen.

von Bashe, Major und Kommandant.

Harry Tate

[illegible] Buchdruckerei in Stralsund.

Rules & Regulations.

1. It is the duty of every prisoner of war to make himself familiar with the Commandants special orders, fixed on the black board on the landing of each barrack, and/or made public at the roll calls.

2. Prisoners of war of all nations are under the German martial law (§ 9 Abs. 4 M.Str.G.)

3. The orders of the Commandant or of the German officers, as well as the orders of the sergeant majors or sergeants in performance of their duty and within their quarters, are to be obeyed, also the orders given by the sentries or soldiers on guard. The latter are instructed to use their arms without hesitation in case of attempted flight or gross disobedience.

4. All prisoners of war have to salute the German officers.

5. It is strictly forbidden for P. o. W. to carry arms, such as swords, big knives, pistols a. s. o., or to wear or to have in possession any clothes other than uniforms and uniform caps.

6. Every P. o. W. has to be present at the two roll calls which are being held daily at 9 a. m. and in the evening between 4 and 10 p. m. according to the season, on the appointed places i. e. on the Great Dänholm in front of barrack 6 and on the Little Dänholm between barrack F. and the eating room. Leave from the roll calls only by special permit of the Commandant.

7. At 8 a. m. everyone except the sick must have left his bed. Anyone feeling sick has to report this to the sergeant in charge of the barrack in the morning.

8. The meals must be taken in the rooms provided therefore, only sick officers may by special permission have brought their meals into their rooms. Breakfast from 7.30 to 8.30 a. m., dinner from 11.30 to 1.30 p. m., supper from 5.30 to 7 p. m.

9. Bedtime is at 10 p. m. From that time all P. o. W. have to stay in their rooms. Visits to other rooms after 10 p. m. are not allowed. It is prohibited to smoke in bed, nor is it allowed to burn candles in the rooms. No loud noise is allowed during nighttime.

10. Prisoners of war are allowed to write 2 letters and 4 postcards, or 6 postcards in all, per month. Correspondence of any kind with the German population and/or with foreigners living in Germany as well as correspondence with P. o. W. in other camps in Germany, Austria Hungaria, Turkey and Bulgaria is strictly prohibited. All correspondence has to be delivered to the Censors through the intermediary of the German Sergeant in charge of the barrack. The outgoing mail is to be handed to them on the 1st., 10th. and 20th. of each month; on other days letters and postcards will not be accepted. Letters and postcards are to be written in plain language, those containing code words, cypher, shorthand, abreviations a. s. o. will be destroyed.

11. The contents of the incoming parcels will be searched through in the post office in the presence of the owner and than delivered against receipt. Prohibited things will be confiscated. Packing material will not be delivered. Tins will be held back and only their contents will be delivered on application.

12. Reports to the German authorities have to be written in German language.

(exceptions are allowed when there is no P. o. W. in the camp able to read or write German.)

13. Every P. o. W. has the right to see the Commandant and bring forward his special wishes, complaints a. s. o. on week days from 11.30 to 12.30 p. m. Those who wish to take advantage of this, have to assemble at 11.30 on the landing in front of the Commandant's office.

14. Visitors to P. o. W. are on no account admitted.

15. The Commandant appoints a Senior for the camp and one for each room, as a rule this will be the officer highest in rank. The seniors will be held responsible to the Commandant for the good behavior of their brother officers, who have to obey their orders.

16. The names of the inhabitants of each room are to be written on a paper fixed on the outside of the door under consecutive numbers. The Names of the Senior and his substitute on top.

17. Every officer is personally responsible for the cleanliness and the tidiness of his room and for all things given to him for his use, such as bed, sideboard, chair a. s. o. The cleaning of the rooms is being done by the orderlies, and doors and windows must be open during cleaning time. At night i. e. after the evening roll call the windows must be shut, only the top windows may be kept open during the night. Open windows are to be secured by the window hoops.

18. Every P. o. W. is being held responsible for any damage caused by him intentionally or carelessly. Slamming of doors is prohibited.

19. It is forbidden to use any part of the things provided for, be it furniture or anything else, but for its proper purpose. Plates, pans coffee-cans, spoons, table knives, forks a. s. o. provided for by the German authorities in the eating rooms and kitchens are not allowed to be taken into the rooms and used there.

20. Careful attention is to be given to the kitchen ranges and stoves, especially to the regulation stoves, while using them.

21. Eatables, which are sent to the P. o. W. or which are being sold in the Canteens may be cooked on the small kitchen ranges, specially provided for in barracks and in the camp, but not in the great camp kitchens.

22. Rod-fishing in the basin between the Great & Little Dänholm is allowed, only on the board of the Little Dänholm. It is strictly forbidden to dig for worms in the park, on the paths and roads, fields, gardens and lawns.

23. It is also forbidden to walk or lie down on the grass, except on the grass between the chief road leading to the exit and the Water basin.

24. Bathing and swimming in the basin is prohibited.

25. It is strictly forbidden to play football, hockey or golf inside the camp or to practice therein.

26. Spitting on the floor of the barracks is forbidden. There are spittoons in the rooms, which serve also for gathering tobacco ashes, ends of cigars and Cigarettes and matches. It is also forbidden to spit through the windows or to throw anything through them.

27. The senior of each room has to see that the Barrack regulations are observed by his brother officers and the orderlies. He is responsible for the good order and cleanliness in his room and will be made liable for any damage. Disobedience to his orders by his brother officers or the orderlies as well as against the Rules he has to report to the German officer in charge of the camp. Having taken over the room, the Senior is responsible for the things therein.

28. All private property is to be kept on the appointed places. It is prohibited to put nails into the walls or doors.

von Bashe, Major and Commandant.

Above: British and Indian long-term or convalescent prisoners of war, as part of an international agreement for neutral internment for such men, arrive in Château d'Oex, Switzerland, for a comfortable measure of freedom there.   *Miss E M Selby*

Opposite: A notice in English and German posted in each room at Stralsund Camp for officer prisoners of war.   *A S Witherington*

Right: Britons arrive in Switzerland from Germany.
                    Miss E M Selby

The King's Message to you.

The Queen and I send our heartfelt greetings to the Prisoners of War of my Army on your arrival in England. We have felt keenly for you during your long sufferings and rejoice that these are ended and that this year brings to you brighter and happier days.

GEORGE R.I.

Above: The scene at the station Château d'Oex.   *Cecil Hart*

Left: Royal greeting to prisoners of war on their return.   *J Hain*

Above: A direct hit has concluded the usefulness of this gun; an incident in the Ypres Salient, Autumn, 1917.   *G M Liddell*

[Diary page, handwritten:] working all night, terrible wounds, doing dressings in a dug out by the aid of a candle, very tired, one death in the night, men groaning & in agony with pain, terrible bombardment all night, shaking the place, never to be forgotten night. Sun 2nd July very tired, relieved off dressings 9 am, just down for a little rest & then called up to go to the trenches to dress wounded & get them back, terrible bombardment on, awful sight in first & second lines, dead bodies laid all over, parts of bodies scattered on trench sides, terrible carnage & slaughter, brought many wounded down, hard & difficult work in the narrow trenches, parts of parapet blown away, dug outs filled with dead & wounded, a terrible smell & many flies, many men unable to be brought in owing to heavy firing, very hard day for all, only had a biscuit or two, feeling the want of food & sleep but still going

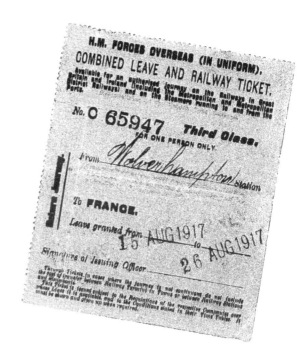

Above left: Stretcher-bearer and medical orderly, Private Ridsdale's work on the first two days of the Battle of the Somme, July, 1916. For 1 July his diary reads: 'First wounded arrive at 8 am. Very busy, wounded coming in by the hundreds, the road to hospital like the way to a football match. A pathetic sight, the men lined up four deep to be dressed'.   *Frank Ridsdale*

Above: Return from leave; Wolverhampton to Le Havre.   *J D Brew*

Left: A soldier's Will, handwritten at the back of his paybook.   *John S Knox*

Opposite above left: Captain Ritchie's bulldog, Arras, Spring, 1917.   *N M McLeod*

Opposite above right: Arras, Spring, 1917 and these three officers of 96 Brigade RFA, McLeod and Bain of D Battery and Ritchie of the Ammunition Column, will have need of their trench waterproof coats for the Battle of Arras which opened with snow on 9 April.   *N M McLeod*

Opposite below: Oppy Wood, June, 1917.   *L G Dickenson*

[Paybook Will page, handwritten:]

18

WILL.

In the event of my death I give the whole of my property and effects to Mrs J. Knox. Folly House West Boldon Newcastle on Tyne.

John S. Knox
Private. No 13616
March 23rd 1915. 6th East Yorkshire Pioneers

Witness
Henry Marshall
L/cpl 6453
6 East Yorkshire

Private note to B/Gen. Lewes (Commdg. 147 Brigade 49 Division)

7/10/17

Dear General,

      My battalion has had an extremely rough time this afternoon and the men are much exhausted with the very wet conditions and heavy shelling (casualties 4 Officers 60 o.r.) To do <u>any</u> justice to themselves they need a night's sleep.   A lot of my equipment and two Lewis guns with many rifles were buried in the mud.

                  J. Walker.

Above: 'To do justice to themselves they need a night's sleep.' A battalion commander's concern for his men during the Third Battle of Ypres (1/5 Duke of Wellington's West Riding Regiment).   *J Walker*

Opposite above: A gunnery officer paints the scene on the eve of the Battle of Messines in June, 1917. In the ensuing battle he was to lose his son.   *E A P Hobday*

Opposite: Gunners extricating a gun from its firing position, Ypres Salient, Autumn, 1917.   *G M Liddell*

Right: Christmas, 1917, and the 36th Ulster Division looks back at the Third Battle of Ypres, at Messines and at Thiepval on the Somme battlefront in the previous year.   *N M McLeod*

Lewis Gunners. Revolver, 2 bombs, 4 magazines per gun.
Stretcher Bearers. 2 prepared waterproof sheets, first aid case.
Bayonet men.   Rifle & bayonet, 50 rounds S.A.A., 2 bombs.

Box respirators will be worn in the alert position.
Equipment will not be worn.
Hands and faces will be blackened, and bayonets painted.
No papers or marks of identification will be carried by raiders.

6. At XERO - 10, raiding party will be formed up in NO MANS LAND
within 150 yards of objective. Tapes will be laid by scouts
from the QUARRY to the forming up place. At ZERO the Artillery
Barrage opens and remains on enemy front line for 5 minutes.
At ZERO the raiding parties will move forward guided by the
scouts to their point of entry.
Artillery Barrage table attached.

7. The signal for withdraw at ZERO plus 30 will be a parachute Green
rocket. A searchlight behind our lines will show the direction
of the withdrawal, also, a machine gun in reserve line firing
dots and dashes will be used for the same purpose.
The withdrawal will be covered by the parapet parties at each
point of entry.

8. GENERAL INSTRUCTIONS. (a) Prisoners will be sent back at once
under escort. It is extremely important to secure letters,
shoulder straps or identity discs.
            Each man must make a point of bringing
back some booty, the best booty is a live prisoner.
            (b) On no account will any of our wounded
or dead be left in enemy's trenches or NO MAN'S LAND.
            (c) All special equipment will be checked
on return.
            (d) Raiding party will be checked and hot
meal and rum served out on return to

9. Battalion Advanced Headquarters will be at QUARRY COY H.Q.
10.Advanced Aid Post will be formed at   QUARRY   DUGOUTS.

11.ZERO hour will be notified later. Watches will be synchronised
at   4   p.m. and a pass word issued to all concerned.

12 ACKNOWLEDGE.

                         Captain & Adjutant.
            1/6th Battn Sherwood Foresters. . . . .

Issued at   by runner:-
Copy No 1   O.C.Raid.   Copy No 2   O.C."A"Party.
  "   " 3   O.C."B"party.   "   " 4   O.C."C"Party
  &   " 5   M.O.   "   " 6   139th Brigade.
  "   " 7   HILL 70 GROUP R.A.   "   " 8   139th M.G.Coy.
  "   " 9   O.C.139th T.M.B.   "   " 10   File.
  "   " 11   War Diary.

1 Nov. 5th 1917.

My dear darling old Johnnie

It is such a thankful old man who is writing to you as I have such a load off my mind & now it is all over I don't think there is any harm in telling you about it. As soon as I got back from leave I learnt that I was down for a raid on the Bosche, so being such a coward I have had the wind up horribly, also being of a cheerful nature I felt a presentiment that I should not return. Now it is all over it has developed into a screaming farce, but my God it was not funny at the time. The ~~reason~~ of the joke is that your old 'un captured a prisoner. I don't know why anyone laughs at this unless it is that I am not famed for my martial spirit. I am awfully bucked with myself & my first thought was won't those two little boys at home be delighted with their daddy. This affair took place at night with our guns & the Hun guns all firing & with shells bursting all round it was like hell loose. My costume for the affair

Opposite and this page: 'The best booty is a live prisoner'. Lieutenant Cooper, B Company, 6th Battalion Sherwood Foresters, receives his order (28 October, 1917) for a trench raid, leads his men in the raid and writes home of its success, adding photographic evidence of his personal coup. *W L Cooper*

Left: 1917 and the Ypres Salient; a September victory for the 11th Battalion West Yorks is remembered at Christmas. *J D Todd*

Below: A wounded soldier leaves a hospital in France. On the back of this card is written a note from one of the nurses to her sister, also a nurse, 'A boy just off to England. Looks happy doesn't he, Alice?' *Alice Dennison*

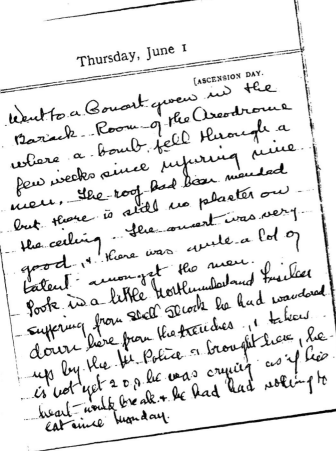

Thursday, June I

[ASCENSION DAY.

*Went to a Concert given in the
Barack Room of the Aerodrome
where a bomb fell through a
few weeks since injuring nine
men. The roof had been mended
but there is still no plaster on
the ceiling. The concert was very
good.* "*There was quite a lot of
talent amongst the men.
Took in a little Northumberland Fusilier
suffering from shell Shock he had wandered
down here from the trenches* "*taken
up by the M. Police & brought here, he
is not yet 2 o.p. he was crying as if his
heart would break & he had had nothing to
eat since Monday.*

Some Swank
after having
Taken
Wancourt
Tower.

A GAME
OF
PATIENCE

Above: 'He was crying as if his heart would break.' A professional nurse (Q.A.I.M.N.S.) gets a shellshock case in her ward (a school in Hazebrouck). His shellshocked condition was shown in a number of ways and could have originated from different causes. In a contemporary account, Lance Bombardier Robinson wrote of dealing with a man deranged by the explosion of a shell nearby. He 'made a most awful noise, turned round gripping me like a drowning man … pointed to his eyes and gripped me like glue'. Robinson could find no wound and tried to carry him to the Field Dressing Station. 'His legs were too weak to walk and he was shaking all over, beads of perspiration showing all over his body.' The man had still gestured that he wanted to take his pals the water he had been carring when the shell exploded. After this he fell into a silence that nothing would break. *Document. Mary Ethel Goldthorp*

This page and over: An R.A.M.C. stretcher-bearer serving with 7th Northumberland Fusiliers captures life in the trenches through a series of cartoons.

Next for
T·A·B

(Injection against Typhoid)

'AL WORS'

When
the
7th NF
Took
8 French Mortars
& Machine
GUNS.

As seen through
the victims eyes

Going out
WIRING.

OH! The loose Trench board

GUNS, ENGINES, MOTORS, ay and
even TANKS can'no stand this
and hav te gan back for Repairs
but heres me, me thats been
out TWO YEARS and I've got
te stick it

FED UP

Above: Self service for servants — batmen of the Divisional Artillery HQ, 25th
Division, in France, 1918.   *N M McLeod*

"*My strength is as the strength of ten Because my heart is pure*"

I RESOLVE by God's Grace, on my return, to be able to look my mother, or sister, or wife or sweetheart in the face, and have in my memory no dark might I would hide from her, and know that I have willingly seen no sight unfit for her pure eyes.

I PRAY that on my marriage or on my return to my wife I may know that I have played the man and acted fairly, and that I may give the same gift of spotless purity that I expect to receive.

I PRAY that I may pass on to my children a blessed heritage of self-control and clean thought that will make their lives also strong and joyous.

"*We are more than conquerors through Him that loved us*".

By God's grace I will conquer !

Signed_____ ART & DAD

Left: Self-control and clean thought by a soldier husband and father — to be achieved 'by God's grace'.   *A Howes*

Opposite: 'With the object of infecting our troops.' An official warning.   *R E Barringer*

Below: 'On no account should you marry until you are cured.' In another document a similiar warning is given by 'We, 1,000 officers, non-commissioned officers and men, patients in a venereal disease hospital at home'.   *J B Bennett*

ADVICE ON DEMOBILISATION.   Form V. 18.

(*The* Government *desires to draw your serious attention to the contents of this leaflet.*)

Venereal Diseases.

There are two chief Venereal Diseases: Syphilis, also known as the Pox or the Bad Disorder; and Gonorrhœa, commonly known as the Clap. Both these diseases are usually the result of impure sexual intercourse.

During demobilisation, and on the way to your home, you may be exposed more than usually to temptations which may lead to sexual intercourse with strangers, whereby you run grave risk of contracting disease.

If you should fail to heed this warning you should seek medical advice at the earliest possible moment after exposure to the risk of infection. By so doing, disease may be entirely prevented, or, it not prevented, a much more rapid cure can be ensured.

Venereal Diseases can only be cured **by early and skilled treatment**. Failure on your part to obtain such treatment may endanger your own health and life as well as the health and life of others.

If you have already received treatment, this should be continued until a doctor certifies that it is no longer necessary. You may still be diseased although you may see no outward signs, and failure to persevere in treatment may lead to very serious results.

You are particularly warned against treating yourself, or going to quacks, herbalists, etc., for treatment. Chemists and druggists are not qualified to treat Venereal Diseases and valuable time may be lost by going to them for medicines.

On no account should you marry until you are cured.

Treatment free of charge under conditions of secrecy can be obtained at practically all the large Hospitals throughout the Country, and a list of some of these Hospitals is printed on the back of this leaflet.

If you are not in one of the towns mentioned in this list, the Medical Officer of Health of your district will advise you confidentially as to the nearest Centre available for free treatment, or the information may be obtained from a police officer.

5786   Wt. 19 94 250   1/66'000   3/19   S.O.   L.B4.

HEADQUARTERS,
24TH
INFANTRY BDE.

No.

Date.

8th Division No. 5/208/A

C. R. A. (20)
C. R. E. (6)
23rd Inf.Bde. (6)
24th Inf.Bde. (6)
25th Inf.Bde. (6)
1/7th Durham L.I. (4)
8th Bn. M.G.C. (5)
A.D.M.S. (4)
8th Div.Train. (5)
8th Div.M.T.Company.
D.A.D.O.S.
D.A.D.V.S.
A. P. M.

8th Div.Reception Camp.
211th Employment Company.
Camp Commandant.

----

(1)   There are a number of women in the recovered area
who have had intercourse with German soldiers and have been infected
with Venereal Disease.

(2)   It should be recollected that before the War Venereal
disease was far more prevalent in GERMANY than in any civilised
country, and it is, therefore, most probable that any woman to whom
German soldiers have had access is contaminated.   Moreover, the
Germans would naturally leave such women behind with the object of
infecting our troops.

(3)   These facts should be brought to the notice of all
ranks and the risk that is run by having intercourse with the
women referred to should be most carefully impressed upon everyone.

                                        Lieut-Colonel.
                        A.A. & Q.M.G. 8th Division.

22.10.18.

11ᵗʰ APRIL
43

pm.
9.30
cont⁴.   Beaudescure side.

10.30   Went into Merville over footbridge
with Col: Scott, his adj: one
sapper (Holland) & 4 infantry.

At one bridge in town which
had failed to fall, we heard
voices. Crept to within 10 yards
& found they were "Boche" throwing
bombs into the houses. We
returned over footbridge & the
Colonel gave orders for it to be
blown up. We had an idea the
enemy were following us & as
the bridge went up, we heard
screams & groans, so
imagined that some Boche
went up with it. As we walked
along canal bank to H.Q. we
heard the enemy keeping pace
with us on opposite bank &
when nearly to H.Q. he opened
fire on us, but we got away.

11.30   Our troops coming in &
manning embankment. Just
had lively M.G. & rifle scrap
with "Boche" on other side of
canal. Our losses 1 killed
8 wounded.

Boche has fired town &
our position is light as day.
midnight His in darkness.
12.30   Retirement complete
except for petrols.

Above: German threatened breakthrough, Merville, April, 1918, and the demolition
of a bridge.   *G M Gahagan*

so many battles. We have had a rather tiring time but rejoice in the knowledge that the Hun has had a very great shock & that the Sons of Odin who wish to live by their "Good German sword" eke out their existence a good bit further East than they did 4 days ago.

Well dear I hope you are well and that I shall see you about the end of September

Above: 'It's a good war now.' A field artillery battery commander expresses delight at the success of the huge counter-attack in August. He goes on to rejoice 'in the knowledge that the Hun has had a great shock and that the sons of Odin who wish to live by their 'Good German Sword' eke out their existence a good bit further East than they did four days ago.
T H G Stamper

Below: 'A map, a revolver, a cup of wine and an old French woman trying to kiss me.' The 16th Battalion Sussex Regiment advance as liberators in October, 1918.
G S Edwards

they all rushed out into the street & kissed everyone!! Some started to kneel down & say prayers in the road, & others I saw the men wine which they had hidden for 4 years!! You would have laughed to see me. I was as usual the leading Company & was trying hard to keep the Coy going in the right direction, & not to get them into view from the Boshe too much & was walking along with a map, a revolver, a cup of wine, & an old French woman trying to kiss me all the time!! It was the most humorous war, as well as the most tragic! There were of course cases of civilians getting wounded & having women & children so near was very disconcerting. We are now in rest in a village close by, & are being treated better than we have ever been since we came abroad. I have got an old woman with

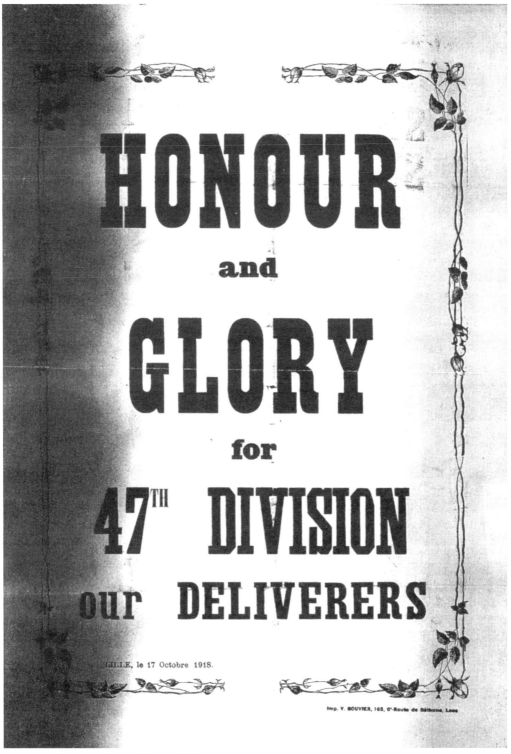

Above: Londoners liberate Lille.   *A St G Colthurst*

Above: Armistice Day in Baghdad — General Marshall reads the proclamation.
V H W Dowson

Below: Munition girls at Barnbow Works, Leeds, learn news of the Armistice.
Leeds City Libraries

Gipsy Hill Training College
40. The Avenue
S.E. 19.

36

Nov: 12ᵗʰ 1918

Dear Mother,

As you say, it seems unbelievable. It is the suddenness of the end which is so staggering. Is'nt it ripping that our men had just reached Mons again before hostilities ceased. The next excitement is how soon the men will be coming back again. Rory should have a good chance of it, I should think, but Jock may have to wait. Fancy all the prisoners being back within a month! But o, it's hard on families like the Inneses, who have no one left to welcome home. You can't help remembering them. . . .

I was going to ask you how the news came to you. I had been working & was just in Miss Anderson's room talking to her when I heard rockets & sirens. We went to the window, & heard maroons. So Bunch & I tore up to the station. On the way flags were being hung out of the windows. Some terrified souls really believed, however, that it was an Air Raid! Others jokingly said so to one another. A dustman over the way waved his hand to us & called out " It's Peace all right this time! Everyone had broad beams on his or her face. Soon the church bells began to ring; otherwise there was very little demonstration in these parts.

After lunch, Miss Houghton, the Eurhythmics teacher, & we felt we simply could not work, so a party of us went up to London to see the sights. Unfortunately it was drizzling steadily. There were masses of people about, but scarcely any disorder. The only rowdiness was made by conglomerate lorry-loads of munition girls, wounded soldiers etc, who rattled along the streets waving flags & blowing "instruments of torture", as Daddy would call them, & yelling excitedly. We actually managed to get into a shop & had an unrestricted pre-War Tea at pre-War prices! Regent St was a blaze of light on the way home, but the other lamps had not

Above: 'The only rowdiness was made by conglomerate lorry-loads of munitions girls, wounded soldiers etc.' Molly Macleod, a teacher-training student at Gypsy Hill College, Twickenham, observes the London Armistice Day celebrations.

M L Macleod

Above: Armistice Day thanksgiving service, Bass Brewery Middle Yard, Burton upon Trent.
Bass Brewery Museum, Burton upon Trent (86.1396)

Below: A Cleveland street party to celebrate the end of the war.
Beamish: The North of England Open Air Museum

No. 1 DISPERSAL CAMP.

NOTICE.

YOU want to get Home quickly.   **WE** want to help you.

Study this carefully and check your own progress.

WHAT HAPPENS.	WHERE.	WHY.
1 Your names are called in the ... ... 2 Your Original and Duplicate Dispersal Certificates are compared. 3 You are separated into Armed and Un-armed parties. 4 You inform a clerk the station you wish to go.	SORTING SHED	1 & 2 To make certain you are the right man 3 To avoid confusion. 4 To speed up train arrangements
1 If you are armed—you are marched to the... and given a sand bag, string and label. 2 You take off your equipment and have it checked and give up any live stuff: Cartridges, bombs, etc. 3 You should take your knife, fork and spoon out of your kit bag and put them in your pocket.	PACKING SHED	1 For packing your private stuff. 2 To see if you have lost anything on the way, or forgotten to leave explosives in France. 3 So as to be able to eat your meals
If you have NOT lost anything on the way, you are marched to the ... ... where you hand in your equipment, rifle and Duplicate Dispersal Certificate.	ORDNANCE HUT	Because the Government want it.
If you HAVE lost anything on the way you are dropped at the	DEFICIENCY HUT	To decide whether you have to pay for it or not.
In both cases you are next taken to the ... and given your ORIGINAL Dispersal Certificate. SEE THAT IT IS THE ORIGINAL.	WAITING HUT	To give you a rest and prevent confusion.
From there you are taken to the ... ... and asked if you will have a suit of clothes or voucher for 52/-	PATTERN ROOM	Because the Government owes it to you.
Then you enter the ... ... and get an OUT of WORK policy from the Ministry of Labour Department.	POLICY OFFICE	So that you will be able to support yourself if you are out of a job.
Next you get a Protection Certificate to show you have been Demobilised, from the	DISPERSAL OFFICE	So that you wont be arrested if you are in uniform without a pass, and to enable you to draw your money whilst on leave.
Then you are paid two pounds (£2) at the ...	PAY OFFICE	Advance on account of credit owing. Paymaster will balance your account later.
1 After that you have your Documents finally checked and receive in ... ... 2 Great Coat Voucher. 3 Ration Book.	FINAL CHECKERS OFFICE	1 To see that no mistakes have been made by the dispersal staff. 2 To enable you to get £1 in exchange when you get home. 3 And food.
Finally you are looked after in ... ... Fed, sent home, and GOOD LUCK TO YOU.	DEPARTURE SECTION	Because you have done your bit.

Above: A suit of clothes because 'the government owes it to you'.   *Liddle Collection*

Opposite above: 1919 and warfare not ended, Britons in North Russia have located and are now destroying a Bolshevik post in forest near Vonga.   *A R Koe*

Opposite below: The occupation of Germany; British troops march through Cologne in 1919: 'The streets ... full of boys who I suppose will grow up to try and conquer the world again'. (E P Neville)   *J C H Willett*

No. 307244 Pte Percy Froude Ward
West Yorkshire Regiment
Served with honour and was disabled in the Great War.
Honourably discharged on 19th June 1919.
George R.I.

Above: A certificate of honour.   *P F Ward*
Below: British gunners with a German heavy howitzer.   *N M McLeod*

QUEEN'S HOTEL,
LEEDS.

Above: Menu for a dinner in Leeds in celebration of the signing of peace in 1919.

S C Marriott

Below: Ex-servicemen take part in the 1919 Victory Parade in Newcastle upon Tyne.

J W Rayner

PEACE DAY MAREHAM-LE-FEN. JULY. 19. 1919.

Above: Peace celebrations, July 1919,
Burton upon Trent.
Bass Brewery Museum, Burton upon Trent

Opposite above: Peace Day, July, 1919, and
the remarkable costumed band of Mareham-
le-Fen, Lincolnshire, a band formed to
celebrate the end of the war and still in
existence today, poses for picture number
one in its history.
Museum of Lincolnshire Life, Lincoln

Opposite below: The Victory Parade, Lime
Street, Liverpool, 1919.   *Liverpool Record Office*

Right: June, 1919, and the Peace Treaty is
signed – the diary of a bereaved financée.
Phyllis Constance Iliff

June 22nd 1919

Peace is signed now
& it means that the
war is over. & my life
with it. Though it may
bring joy to thousands
yet — to those breaking
hearts it means the end
of all things
    Oh! I wish I was
dead !!!

Above: A land fit for heroes, but for this ex-soldier wearing his medal ribbons it is eviction for his family from a tied cottage at Fulstow Brick Pits near Louth, Lincolnshire.   *Museum of Lincolnshire Life, Lincolnshire*

Opposite: A Federation for Servicemen and its certificate of membership.
         B A McConnell

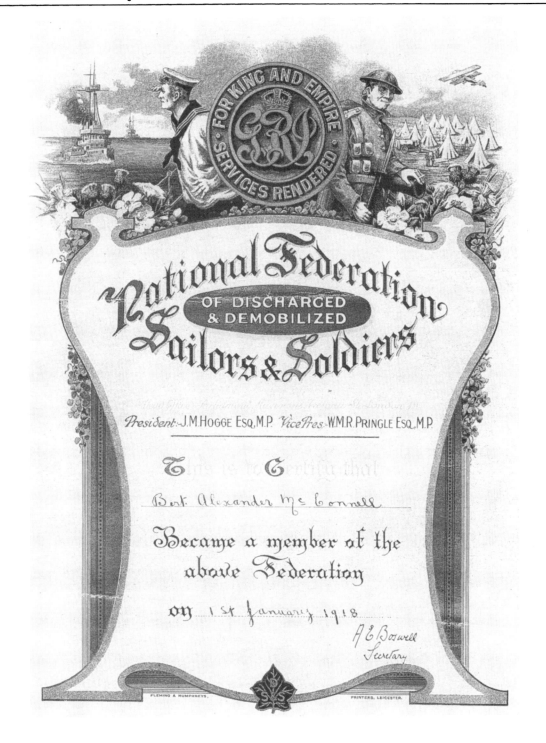

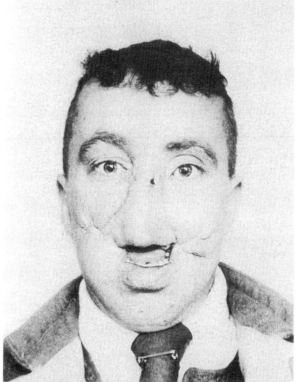

Above: Dedication service at the war memorial, St John's Church, Glastonbury, opposite Goodson's shop, to which one soldier would not return (see page 128).   *H W Goodson*

Left: For some a lasting legacy; Private Bell faces the future. He has been photographed in France, his wounds patched up, the defects closed without regard given to the amount of tissue loss. The first priority at St Mary's Hospital, Sidcup, for Bell's surgeon (Mr Gillies of later fame) would be to undo the scars so that tissue would regain its original position and then plan surgery to fill in the gaps with 'grafts, flaps and pedicles'.

Frognal Centre for Medical Studies, Sidcup

BIRMINGHAM GAZETTE,

WEDNESDAY, 10 DECEMBER, 1919.

MEMORY OR MOCKERY?

[To THE EDITOR OF THE BIRMINGHAM GAZETTE.]

Sir,—Your leader describes the Trades Council's protest as belated and narrow-minded. The former circumstance is accounted for by virtue of the fact that the proposal only recently came before our notice. From the very day when one of our members (who was, by the way, existing in a garret on just over £1 a week) received an invitation to subscribe to the proposed Hall of Memory, we took objection to it and utilised the earliest occasion to bring our feelings before the public.

As regard our narrowness of mind, it is very easy to develop in this direction after four years active service, and easier still to let the weakness overcome one when confronted by such a proposal as to waste nearly half a million pounds worth of building materials and labour on an edifice which can serve no useful purpose, whilst demobilised men, their widows and orphans, are huddled together in garrets or drifting into the workhouse.

You state that "here is a chance for all who are concerned for the beauty of the city." Certainly it is, but surely Floodgate-street and Summer-lane require beautifying before we think of improving the neighbourhood of Victoria-square, and I should also like to point out in conclusion that it is in such neighbourhoods as the former that we find the broken-hearted widows and starving kiddies of the men whose sacrifice made it possible for the city of Birmingham to retain that sufficiency of glorious buildings which it possesses at the present day. I still maintain that a garden city where the sufferers of the war might dwell in peace would be a much more noble and fitting appreciation of what this city thinks of her heroes.—Yours, etc.,

C. E. LEATHERLAND
(ex-Coy. Sergt.-Major),
President N.U. Ex-Service Men
(Birmingham Branch).

6

abled ex-Servicemen, who might otherwise have been committed to prison. In one case the Society saved a mentally disabled ex-Serviceman from going to penal servitude, and I will mention that Mr. Justice Roche on one occasion at the Gloucester Assizes expressed his obligation to the Society for the help it had given him in dealing with a difficult case.

Asylum Cases.

Various asylums have been visited during the year and seventy-six cases dealt with. Many have received assistance in connection with their appeals for pensions. Advice has been given them and their families. Employment has also been found for a few discharged cases.

The General Secretary himself deals with ex-Servicemen at Broadmoor Criminal Lunatic Asylum, where there are, I am sorry to say, about one hundred ex-Servicemen. I understand his frequent visits to that institution are welcomed by the Medical Superintendent and the inmates, who feel that, although they are isolated from their families, they have a friend in the Ex-Services Welfare Society. I would like to thank the Home Office and its officials for their courtesy to the Society at all times.

Here is a typically sad case which will indicate to you how helpful the Society can be to these ex-Servicemen. An ex-Serviceman has been in Broadmoor Asylum since 1922. He had not received a visit from his wife during the whole of the five years although she wrote frequently. The General Secretary interviewed the wife and found that she was an invalid and was unable to travel by train. She was persuaded to visit her husband and the Society arranged that she should be taken to see him in a conveyance.

I would also like to mention that every ex-Serviceman at Broadmoor received a large packet of cigarettes from the Society at Christmas.

Financial Assistance and Relief.

It has already been mentioned that over £2,000 has been spent on relief and assistance and ex-gratia payments. It must be remembered that when an ex-Serviceman is taken as a patient to this Society it is considered as part of the curative treatment that he should be relieved of his domestic anxieties, and I must thank those members of the Committee who have devoted their time to visiting the homes and families and made recommenda-

Above left: 'Demobilised men, … widows and orphans are huddled together in garrets or drifting into the Workhouse.' One ex-servicemen's organization stands opposed to the way the City of Birmingham intends to commemorate the war service and sacrifice of its citizens.   *C E Leatherland*

Above right: Life sentence: permanent, semi-permanent or temporary mental derangement. Paragraphs from the 1926 Annual Report of the Ex-Services Welfare Society. This Society, under the name of 'Combat Stress', is still, in 1994, supporting a 1914-1918 serviceman.
'Combat Stress' with Ex-Services Mental Welfare Society
West Yorkshire Archive Service, Wakefield

Above: The magnetism of past experience of comradeship in shared danger. Three men of the Manchester Regiment did not wait long to get back to France. January, 1919, and Clement Fletcher, M. K. Burrows and Phil Fletcher reach the entrance to 'Brickstack Fort', Cuinchy.   *M K Burrows*

Below: Sad faces here but a positive legacy of the Great War experience. Wartime comradeship has led to fifty years of civilian fellowship sustaining the spirit through whatever the years may have held. This 1968 photograph shows men at the last formal meeting of the Fife Gallipoli Club in St Andrews. In 1994, seventy-nine years after the campaign, there are still veterans of the Dardanelles and the Gallipoli Peninsula in the Gallipoli Association.   *A Brown*

AN INDEX OF PERSONS AND PLACES

Initials and rank given as in the text or documents illustrated